GARY

Hope you enjoy the Read

Keep up the "1.Pump"

Your a Great Friend.

Enjoy the Photo Album

"What a Amazing Year

We Had.

Kevin Yule

Oct 2013

# INTERNAL
## PUMPTITUDE

## *INTERNAL PUMPTITUDE*

### *Our WHY:*

Everything we do will challenge the status quo. We will go to places we have never been before. As a result, we will never want to go back. Our vision and mission is to clearly differentiate ourselves from others, along with having the need to constantly and never-endingly improve. We strive to be smart, hungry and humble, and live with purpose, drive and style. We promote and inspire others, and we live to make a difference.—Art Van Leadership Team

*— 68 ways to UNLEASH your —*

# INTERNAL PUMPTITUDE

## INSPIRE, GROW *and* BECOME MORE

# BY KIM YOST

## With Donna Yost and Linda Dessau

Life 2000 Ltd.
1583 Heronwood Court
Bloomfield Hills, Michigan 48302

Library of Congress Control Number: 2013917236

ISBN-13: 978-1-4675-8291-9

First printing, September 2013

Printed in Canada

# CONTENTS

# FOREWORD

## Mike Lipkin

My name is Mike Lipkin, and I am a motivational speaker. That is all I do. I talk about how to be inspired and how to inspire other people under any circumstances.

Kim Yost is a motivational speaker, but that is just a sidebar to what he does. Kim is really a motivational doer. He is a person of action, a person of vision and a person of warmth. He packs as much into a day as the average person packs into a career.

Whether it's writing a book every year, leading a highly successful chain of retail stores, or starting new businesses, Kim has both the intuitive genius and the expertise to achieve the impossible. He just "gets it" and he has the ability to communicate his secrets of success in a way that everyone can understand.

Kim writes like he is talking to you directly. You can feel his enthusiasm. You can hear his passion. You can understand his methods. Best of all, you can apply his recipe for success. Since I met Kim two years ago, I have consistently implemented ideas from *Pumptitude* and *Maximum Pumptitude*. On almost every occasion, I achieved my objectives.

The ultimate attribute of highly successful achievers is their ability to choose their attitude irrespective of their situation. They thrive on disruption and uncertainty because their confidence comes from within. They believe they'll find a way, and their belief becomes self-fulfilling. Most importantly, they are consistent in their actions. They achieve the impossible time after time. But for these high achievers, it's not the impossible; it's their standard. That's why they become the standard by which others are judged.

In *Internal Pumptitude*, Kim Yost takes you deep into the mind of a champion high achiever. He shares stories with you that will make you laugh and cry with amazement. But in every story, there is a principle that will take your personal effectiveness to the next level. There is no fluff in this book. Kim doesn't have time for that. He doesn't tolerate it in others either.

*Internal Pumptitude* is an easy, fast-paced read. It will only take you a few hours to read, but you will want to read it over and over again. My only request of you is that you pay it forward. Share what you've learned. Live by example. Develop your own *Pumptitude* principles. You may change not only your life, but the lives of everyone around you as well.

Take the first steps and life will partner with you to take you as far as you want to go. I'm envious of you. You have a treat in store. Read it and reap.

Mike Lipkin

Art Van Elslander, Mike Lipkin, Gary Van Elslander and Kim Yost

# ACKNOWLEDGMENTS

A special note of appreciation and gratitude to the following one percenters and high achievers who have added so much richness to I-Pump. Wow, thanks so much to all of you for taking the time and effort to contribute!

1. Dennis Archer Jr. (Chapter 9: Relationships)
2. Diane Charles (Chapter 3: #16)
3. Troy Davis (Chapter 5: Habits)
4. Cathy DiSante (Chapter 6: Creativity is a Curse)
5. Michelle Dolski (Chapter 1: 68-Day Challenge)
6. Julie Donegan (Chapter 11: #58)
7. Colin Donnelly (Chapter 8: Inspire Others)
8. Gary Duncan (Chapter 12: The Ultimate Reward)
9. Amelia Ellenstein (Chapter 3: One Percenters)
10. Kevin Gilfillan (Chapter 7: Embrace Change; Chapter 8, #39; Chapter 12, #62)
11. Bob Hooey (Chapter 2: Say Yes, You Can)
12. Jack Krasula (Chapter 11: Life Chest)
13. Mike Lipkin (Foreword and throughout the book)
14. Florine Mark (Chapter 3: One Percenters)
15. Josef Miko (Chapter 7: #36)
16. Sandra Miko (Chapter 8: #40)
17. Oscar Miskelly (Chapter 4: No Fear)
18. Ruth Sinawi (Chapter 2: Say Yes, You Can)
19. David Van (Chapter 1: 68-Day Challenge)
20. Gino Wickman (Chapter 10: Uncommon Leadership)
21. Ashley Yost (Chapter 11: #58)

## ADL Award – June 13, 2013

KIM YOST
CEO, Art Van Furniture

# LEADER, MENTOR, COACH & FRIEND

You bring out the best in all of us!
Congratulations on this well-deserved award.

FROM ALL YOUR FRIENDS AT ART VAN FURNITURE

artvan.com

# PRAISE

Of all the comments and emails we received, none have captured the enthusiasm of a reader as well as the following. One of my associates passed along this photo from her girlfriend who was heading off to her wedding. She posted a photo on Facebook of the carry-on she had packed for her honeymoon. Her post joked about how the bag was full of shoes, but more telling was the image of the two books, *Pumptitude* and *Maximum Pumptitude*, propped up against the lid of the suitcase. She wasn't about to get married and go on her honeymoon without getting pumped up! Here's what she had to say:

> *I read in Kim's book that, "Millions of people wake up every morning and say that they want change," and I can say that I have been among those millions at many times in my life, in many different areas of my life. What better place to make change and take an interest in changing than [by] making a commitment with your new husband on your way to your honeymoon, with a suitcase full of your favorite shoes and great personal development books that a great friend recommended. Pumptitude and Maximum Pumptitude are exactly what I needed to FIRE UP.*

*As the general manager of Bay Athletic Club in Alpena, MI, and as an owner of my own Beachbody Health and Fitness business, I have learned how important personal development is. You can only grow as a leader when you continuously learn. If you aren't learning, you are dying as a leader.*

*I do not know Kim personally, but I feel like his books were meant to be in my life at this time. The books were amazing, and my top takeaways were:*

*1. Finding your Power Hour—with the 23-hour day, you can have that one hour for YOU! Use this hour to find your commitment to yourself, your goals, and your drive. It only takes one hour and this is what can move you forward and drive your needle.*

*2. Commitment and the Power of the Third Really. People may be interested with just one "really," but they are really committed with that third "really." I've learned that you must work with the people who are as driven as you. If people are only interested, move forward and work with the willing.*

*3. Never stay satisfied with mediocre, also known as 5,000 ft. The most successful people keep climbing to the 30,000 ft. mark. Stay hungry for your goals, and you'll keep climbing. Don't take that foot off the accelerator, and you'll reach success in all areas of your life.*

*Walking the beach and talking about this book with my husband really helped our relationship as newlyweds. Relationships are so important for success, and communication is so important in relationships. These books create great conversations that nurture and feed our personal and professional lives. As a couple, we now have reasons to aim higher and work harder. We have goals. We have dreams. We "really,*

*really, really" WILL create the best life possible for ourselves.*

*I will use the 68 ways in this book to have a great marriage and a great life. Listen, absorb and take action—that is all you need.*

**Tracie Werblow Granata**, *GM, Bay Athletic Club*

*This past weekend I had a chance to read Maximum Pumptitude. I was honored to see my name in the book and especially on the same page as Cindy Crawford! After reading Maximum Pumptitude, I was pleasantly surprised to gain so many additional insights because I thought Pumptitide was so comprehensive. The perspective by Sandra Miko on "Walking with Purpose" hit a cord with me. I tend to assess a company by the way employees walk around. In a dynamic company, employees walk with purpose; whereas in a static company, the pace is much slower. Congratulations on another success and one that is so meaningful and helpful to its readers.*

**Ralph Stern**, Successful Entrepreneur, owner of Paul's TV of California

*It's incredibly interesting to read Mr. Yost's books as a member of Stage 2 in life. I see an uncharted path with a new level of structure and foundation. It's daunting to begin processing the length of such a long road and start understanding how much there still is to know, but Mr. Yost encouraged me to concentrate on what I already know, not what I don't. My foundation is built*

*and now my instincts can guide me when concrete answers are out of reach.*

*The growing I've done as a result of strong mentorship from Mr. Yost has not come without cost. I have pushed my limits, over-engaged and struggled to balance academics and outside interests. At times, these hurdles have forced me to confront bigger and harder questions than I've felt ready to tackle ... and those are the times I've had to turn back to the instincts triggered by the foundation I built in Stage 1. I am forever better for having faced those questions.*

*Since he has entered my life, I've worked four different jobs, worked on a start-up venture of my own, and maintained new drive and ambition in my architectural studies at the University of Michigan. Gratitude will not repay the debt I owe; the only way is to someday do for someone else what he has done for me.*

**Adam Wells**

*Diane Adam's mom* ☺

*I have just spent the last four hours reading Maximum Pumptitude. It's fabulous. I feel as though I've had an inspiration transfusion. Every page held an "AHA" for me. I feel like you invited me to step into your world and accelerate my velocity of gratitude, sharing, learning, and love.*

*I especially like:*

1. *The cycle of self-improvement*
2. *Being smart, hungry and humble*
3. *Going vertical not horizontal*
4. *DxVxF>R*

5.  Love what you hate

6.  Combine thought with action—the power of competition. I love the story of Home Show Canada and opening six stores in one day in Montreal

7.  The thank you walk

8.  Reputation versus character

9.  The man I am versus the man I could be

10. The six stages of life

    You and I are living proof that we're only as good as the people who push us to do more.

    Here's a jewel I've created especially for you: **We can build Self-Discipline by ourselves but we can only build Stretch-Discipline with others.** That's when we do things we would never have done without someone else's help.

    Thank you for all your references to me in the book. Thank you for four precious hours of maximum learning and enjoyment. I will pay it forward.

**Mike Lipkin**, motivational speaker and author

I just returned from Montreal and Minneapolis, trying to schlep some wares and found the copies of Maximum Pumptitude, which you promised. I went to get a Starbucks and turned the first page. I'm not trying to pumptitude your ego, I'm just being honest. I turned every page, enjoying each story, each motivational reminder, new quotes, old quotes. The read was very enjoyable and motivating. As I read, I could hear your voice, almost as if I [were] listening to an audio book. You taking the time to put these stories together and *share what makes you tick is a treasure. Both books will go into my Life Chest, and when I miss you, I can read a few chapters and "listen" to you share your wisdom. Great job!!!*

**Colin Donnelly**, former senior vice-president of merchandising of The Brick Group

*Congratulations on another terrific book! It is like crack. Once I started reading it, I couldn't put it down. You have distilled so many great ideas for success and happiness in one place (again!) that I don't know where to start. I have always known, from way back in the Woodward days, that you are one of the best executives of your generation. With these books and articles, you continue to demonstrate your quality of thinking and acting over and over. It is a delight working with you. I hope to see you again soon.*

**Brian Tracy**, leading self-development author

*Continuous and never-ending improvement. Just one of the many valuable takeaways I gleaned from Pumptitude. I read the first book en route to Greenville, SC to see our Michelin client. The simple approach you took in introducing the book's many important lessons, coupled with your colorful anecdotes, made it a very pleasant read. I wish my law school books were as interesting!*

*My team, wife, and friends would all suggest that I am ADD to a greater or lesser extent. Many of your lessons were about focus. Top of the list was writing*

*down the five things you want to do today. Today was day one of me implementing this. I cannot tell you how many times I have had in my mind what I wanted to get done, then I get to the office, team members start coming in to talk, the phone rings, emails back up, and the tasks move to tomorrow, then tomorrow, etc. I am confident that committing my five to writing will help.*

*Thank you so much for giving me the books. I have already passed Pumptitude to a team member and will continue to do so throughout our executive team. I would love for you to speak to my staff at some point. I will be reading Maximum Pumptitude as soon as I get it back from Dean and will also investigate some of the books in your suggested reading list.*

**Dennis Archer**, president & CEO of Ignition Media Group

*I wish to thank you for your new book Maximum Pumptitude. I have a tendency to start reading your books by lesson randomly and then read from the beginning to the end and then again by lesson from time to time. So now I am all over the Maximum Pumptitude lessons. My general impression is that this book has finer and deeper lessons, covering some that are less talked about. I believe you could write a whole book about some of them. One example is #37, "Cut your losses," where you are addressing a critical issue that in my view has been the root cause of the demise of a number of Fortune 500 companies, such as Xerox, Kodak, Research in Motion, and Best Buy, in the recent past. They are all burdened by leadership who "fail to make decisions, tend to suffer from panic, prejudice, extreme uncertainty, procrastination, over-complexity and over-rationalization."*

*In a time where we are faced with information overflow, it is critical that, "One skill we all have to learn is how to discern between all the information that flows our way (#36)," and that "our goal is to think far more simply and find greater clarity in making our decisions. We must realize that if they're not the right one, we can adjust our course and quickly move in another direction (#37).*

*I enjoy reading the lessons; each one resonates profoundly and deserves pondering deeply.*

**Hossein Chehrzad**, former vice president of Future Shop, consultant to Fortune 500 companies

*Oscar joins me in thanking you both for the copies of Pumptitude and Maximum Pumptitude! He is reading one, and I the other, enjoying all the life tidbits and motivational enthusiasm. They're grand.*

**Carolyn G. Goodman**, mayor, Las Vegas, Nevada

*Let me begin by saying that I was very inspired in reading both of your books. Let me also say that it was a truly extraordinary experience being able to see you speak at the 2013 Las Vegas furniture market at the FMG Symposium. Thank you for all that you've already given me. It has taken me to new heights in both my personal and occupational life. Sincerely, thank you. In an odd way, I almost feel as if you've already begun to mentor me through your books. You're an inspiration to me as a fellow retail man, and as a lifelong learner.*

**Jon Gadbois**, director of marketing, Boston Inc.

# DEDICATION

I dedicate this book to Mr. Art Van Elslander and the entire Art Van leadership team, who continue to grow and evolve into amazing individuals and North America's finest home furnishing retailers.

A note of special appreciation and love to my daughter Ashley and my wife Donna for putting up with me. Oh, and I don't want to forget Linda Dessau, who put up with me every Schmonday as we wrote these three books, and Sandra Miko, my associate at Art Van, who has to deal with me *every* day.

My last shout out goes to Mike Lipkin, my CEO coach and chief motivator and educator. Mike's fingerprints are all over this book, and his enthusiasm and inspiration were instrumental to its completion.

Kim Yost and Art Van Elslander

# INTERNAL PUMPTITUDE

## — Introduction —

# THE ULTIMATE QUESTION

In my first two books, *Pumptitude* and *Maximum Pumptitude*, we talk a lot about external motivation and some of the coaches, authors and speakers who are vested in inspiring, firing up and pumping up the people in their reach. Indeed, a huge percentage of our population relies heavily on them.

Millions of people will attend seminars, read books, watch movies, listen to music, talk to friends and relatives, and seek countless other external motivators. Worse yet, others will go the other way—towards alcohol or illegal drugs. They're all looking for the same thing—something outside to stimulate and motivate them. So when we finished *Pumptitude* and *Maximum Pumptitude*, there remained an important unanswered question:

*How do you find the internal drive and ambition, and then unleash this ultimate I-Pump (internal pumptitude) every day for the rest of your natural life?*

There is a small group of people who already do this. We call them one percenters because they represent the top one percent of achievers in the world. This doesn't mean they don't learn and benefit from the knowledge, motivation and inspiration of others, but they get up every morning with their own battery pack and fire themselves up. My wife Donna, for example, starts and attacks every day with incredible positive energy.

What is it about these one percenters, these top-graders, who have I-Pump in their DNA? How do they manage to inspire everybody who they come in contact with? How can you?

I'm convinced that, deep inside, we all have internal pumptitude. Our goal with *Internal Pumptitude* is to convert as many people from the other 99 percent as possible by helping them learn and understand how to unleash their own I-Pump, as well as continue to inspire and share with others.

**Internal pumptitude (I-Pump): The discovery that you are gifted → a determination to make the most of that gift → an altitude of attitude that is multiplied by the fire within → an inner courage that makes you unstoppable → a passion for the grind → heightened productivity irrespective of circumstances → a plethora of possibilities → a contagious motivation that inspires others → a relentless movement to greatness that feeds on itself and guarantees a great life.**

People who rely regularly on external motivation lack the ability to inspire themselves and others. They are the ones who fall off after the first really on many things that they *want* to do.

What do I mean by the first really? In my first book, *Pumptitude*, I shared the concept of the "Power of the Third Really" (Chapter 5), explaining that billions of people wake up every morning and only get to the first really, e.g., "I really want to lose weight," or "I really want to get a better job." And they **do nothing**.

Millions and millions of people might get to the second really, e.g., "I really, really want to get healthier," or "I really, really want a better future." And they get done about **half** of what they want done.

Then there are the remaining one percenters who get to the third really, e.g., "I really, really, really **will** live out my vision of peak health," or "I really, really, really **will** maximize my true potential and keep going from there." They get **everything done** that they set out to do.

I took this idea further in *Maximum Pumptitude*, revealing the "tyranny of the WANT" (Introduction, #1, "Embrace the Genius of the WILL"). Just saying that you WANT something is to live in a dream world. Saying that you WILL do something is a commitment. This book is a handbook for success for those who WILL put many of its principles into action.

In *Internal Pumptitude*, you will meet several outstanding authors, professional speakers, and high achievers. You've already met my CEO coach, Mike Lipkin, and you'll hear much more from him. You'll also be introduced to authors Gary Ryan Blair, Charles Duhigg, Rick Pitino and others, and an amazing individual named Jim Rohn.

An exciting new feature of this book is that at the end of each chapter we'll introduce you to actual pumped up, extraordinary one percenters, and you'll read their stories about how they live out some of the ideas we presented in that chapter. We'll also connect you with some additional online resources at www. pumptitude.com.

It is so important to invest in your self-development at an early age and continue that investment throughout your life. It took me way too long in my early 20s to truly understand the power of my own personal development, and I don't want that to happen to you. When I look back on my life, I'm constantly reminded of the importance key people have played in my personal and professional development:

Yvonne Nordstrom (my mother), Nana and Papa (my grandparents), Uncle Jim (my godfather), Papa Tony (my adopted father), Uncle David (the inventor you met in *Pumptitude*), several key friends, bosses and professional advisors that include Brian Tracy, Denis Zuccato, Bill Comrie, Ron Barbaro, Art Van Elslander, and too many others to mention. When I *did* realize the power of personal accountability and professional development, it took my life, my career and my family on a path of amazing challenges and successes.

Throughout my 35 rewarding years of working with thousands of individuals, I have seen that everyone has the potential to be a self-motivator and self-starter. I have been delighted to see that with some I-Pump coaching and motivation in place, people were able to achieve things that they didn't believe were possible. I want this for you as well.

In this last book of our trilogy, *Internal Pumptitude*, we will share learning that will enlighten and trigger your own explosive growth potential, empowering you to:

- get challenged and fired up
- adopt new habits and behaviors
- learn from extraordinary one percenters and high achievers
- continue on your never-ending quest to unleash your ultimate internal pumptitude
- learn more of my key life lessons

So as we set upon this amazing ride, once again we ask:

**Are you ready?**

# — Chapter 1 —

# THE 68-DAY CHALLENGE

*Achieving your goals is like a plane taking off from the tarmac; it requires incredible energy to leave the ground, but once you hit that cruising height, the energy is effortless.* —Kim Yost

The 68-Day Challenge was inspired by Gary Ryan Blair, his book *Everything Counts!* and his 100-Day Challenge that happened in the final 100 days of 2012. Gary's concept was that no matter where you finish in a marathon, everybody sprints once they see the finish line ahead. There is something very important about those 100 yards before the finish line, so his challenge was designed to help people finish strong at the end of each year.

Although I agree with Gary's "finish strong" approach, I also feel that by starting strong at the beginning of the year with an amazing vision and mission, which gives you the benefit of a huge kick-start, you set your flight path with a high probability of achieving your year's goals and highest performance.

Since there are 365 days in a year, 68 days represents approximately 20 percent of the year. According to Pareto's Law (also known as the 80/20 rule), 20 percent of our efforts will lead to 80 percent of our results.

At Art Van, we decided that to make a stellar year of success in 2013, we needed to kick it off with a tremendously successful first 20 percent of the year. Therefore, we developed and implemented the first ever 68-Day Challenge.

Here's how it all got started:

From an initial meeting in mid-December 2012 to the project launch in January 2013, the leadership team pulled together in extraordinary ways to make this happen. As Michelle Dolski, director of education and training at Art Van, recalls:

> *Well, I am certainly busy and have lots of projects going on to help develop 3,000 associates across the company. When Kim pulled me in to discuss this new project, I'm thinking, "Oh my God, how do I fit this all in?" But listening to Kim describe his vision in that 45 minutes inspired me and reminded me that this is the work I should be focused on. My position exists to ensure we have people at maximum engagement and achieving peak performance levels. It's not just about the business, though. Kim really cares about the people at Art Van and their development.*

Michelle thought the coolest things about the 68-Day Challenge were these seven phases:

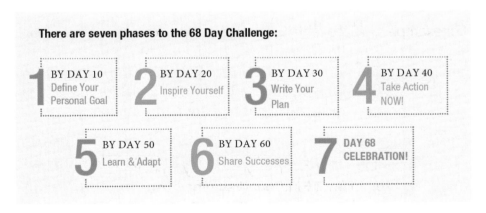

There are seven phases to the 68 Day Challenge:

1 BY DAY 10 — Define Your Personal Goal

2 BY DAY 20 — Inspire Yourself

3 BY DAY 30 — Write Your Plan

4 BY DAY 40 — Take Action NOW!

5 BY DAY 50 — Learn & Adapt

6 BY DAY 60 — Share Successes

7 DAY 68 — CELEBRATION!

**Phase 1: Define Your Personal Goal:** In this phase we go back to the simple assessment tool I introduced in *Pumptitude*, Chapter 1, #9. Draw a circle that is divided into eight different areas of your life: health, wealth, family & friends, playtime & hobbies, home, career/job, relationships, and contribution/spirituality.

First you will rate each area—how are you doing now in that part of your life? Next, make a list of the areas you can enhance. Finally, pick one or two areas of your life to focus on over the next 68 days.

**Phase 2: Inspire Yourself:** Set yourself up for success by incorporating inspiration time into your schedule. Take time every single day to read educational and inspirational material—even if it's just for 20 minutes, then longer on Schmonday when you have more time. You'll hear more about Schmonday in Chapter 5, #22.

Another part of Phase 2 is to come up with a set of SMART goals for each of your areas of focus. A SMART goal is:

**S**pecific
**M**easurable
**A**ttainable
**R**elevant
**T**ime-Bound

For example, "I will go from 150 pounds to 140 pounds by March 9th."

**Phase 3: Write Your Plan:** Now that you have SMART goals in place, write down three things that you will do, change or develop to meet your objectives.

**Phase 4: Take Action Now!** To stay motivated and accountable, keep a copy of your goals and planned actions handy at all times. Schedule actions into your daily and weekly rhythms, along with reminders. Find buddies who are also committed to this process and meet regularly to support each other and spur each other on.

**Phase 5: Learn and Adapt:** Constantly seek to improve your efforts by looking at what's working and what isn't. Acknowledge your "wins" (what went great?), "fixes" (what will you change?) and "ah-hahs" (what can you learn from and how can you inspire others?). Write a list of anything you need to adjust in order to meet your goals.

**Phase 6: Share Successes:** Talk to people in your different life circles about what you've accomplished. You never know who you will inspire and how far your message can spread.

**Phase Seven: Celebration:** Congratulate yourself for being a one percenter—someone who doesn't wait for things to happen, but someone who makes things happen. Celebrate any failures as much as any successes; simply by trying you are a winner.

I was already using this model with entrepreneurs and executives, now it was Michelle's job to take this process to individual leaders and team members throughout our company.

We knew we couldn't force a program like this on anyone, so Michelle's team went to work designing materials that would engage individuals and get them excited about being a leader in their own lives, regardless of their position in the company.

We also saw that if you model and talk about the behavior you want to see, just how many people will want to follow you. Michelle adds, "From six people gathered together in Kim's office, to hundreds of associates and leaders who signed up for the 68-Day Challenge. For the first year, it's a good start!"

The most common goals were about eating healthier, weight loss, exercise, or quitting smoking. My own 68-Day Challenge included getting off Diet Pepsi and replacing it with a glass of water. We'll learn more about these life-changing habits in Chapter 5.

Michelle set her own health and fitness goals as well as financial goals that saw her and her husband Drew (you met Drew in Chapter 8 of *Maximum Pumptitude*) coming up with their own "2013 Gamebook" for home and putting together a plan called

"Project Freedom" to keep them on track to hit new financial goals for the year.

Miraculous things continued to happen at Art Van as more and more people signed onto the challenge and started making significant changes in their lives. They all wanted to turbo-charge their year with this process. People were eating healthier foods and working out when they never had before.

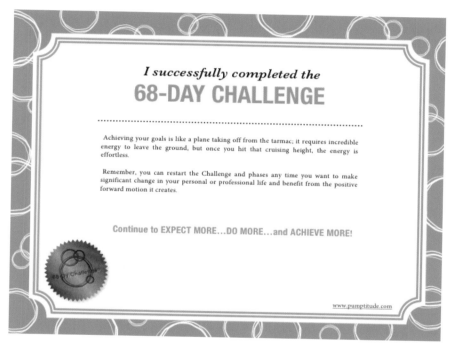

*I successfully completed the*

## 68-DAY CHALLENGE

Achieving your goals is like a plane taking off from the tarmac; it requires incredible energy to leave the ground, but once you hit that cruising height, the energy is effortless.

Remember, you can restart the Challenge and phases any time you want to make significant change in your personal or professional life and benefit from the positive forward motion it creates.

Continue to EXPECT MORE...DO MORE...and ACHIEVE MORE!

www.pumptitude.com

## Are you up for the 68-Day Challenge?

You only need two things to begin the 68-Day Challenge: a pulse and the ability to draw a breath. If you're alive and breathing, you can get on with the 68-Day Challenge.

You can take the 68-Day Challenge as an individual or with your team. By firing up your team with a great simple yearly plan, which you'll read about later in this chapter, you're assured of alignment and clarity of the year's goals.

The New Year is a great time to start the 68-Day Challenge, but you can also go through these seven phases any time you want to make significant change in your personal or professional life and benefit from the positive forward motion it creates.

In Chapter 7, #36, you will read about a great book called *Changeology* and five behaviors that will unlock some new thinking about personal change. You can use this learning directly in your 68-Day Challenge.

Here are some key things to remember about the 68-Day Challenge:

- Completing the 68-Day Challenge, year after year, will give you a life of CANI—constant and never-ending improvement (*Pumptitude*, Chapter 5, #28).

- The Challenge is like a defibrillator to get you back on track, intended to push you out of your comfort zone and give you the power to turn the impossible into the possible.

- One of the most important parts of the challenge is to develop a new attitude. Remember, ***attitude determines altitude*** (*Pumptitude*, Chapter 2).

- The 68-Day Challenge plan is like a seed. When you plant it today, it creates the harvest of tomorrow; if you develop good habits, you will get the compounding effects and benefits. You'll read more about compounding benefits in Chapter 5, #25.

- You are guaranteed one result from the 68-Day Challenge, if properly executed, and that is *impact.*

Consider the Olympics. Without the Olympics to motivate an athlete, they wouldn't be nearly as driven to improve. We all need a big event that inspires us to become more, do more and achieve more. We need to have a dream with a deadline. Without a deadline, people will procrastinate on taking action and waste their precious training time. We need to set ourselves big goals so we can achieve big things.

Taking the 68-Day Challenge is all about recognizing a goal, pushing yourself to new limits, planning for that new level, taking action and improving along the way. This is how I live my life, and I strongly encourage you to live yours the same way. As Mike Lipkin says, "If you don't take care of the tree, you won't be able to enjoy the fruit." I love this quote! To build a strong tree for the future, you must prune it, water it, fertilize it, and give it lots of sunshine.

The 68-Day Challenge is my movement to help everyone achieve their ultimate best. We will be unstoppable. Will you join me?

Visit www.pumptitude.com to download your own 68-Day Challenge worksheet and Certificate of Completion today! These resources, especially the personal worksheet, will give you a laser focus that lasts.

## Art Van 68-Day Challenge Success Stories

At Art Van, we're prepared for an exponential increase in participants for the 68-Day Challenge every year, as people witness the impact it has had on others. I'm going to share just a few examples of the many miracles we saw. First, we have someone who set a very common health goal—to quit smoking. Then, you will read more life-changing stories that will inspire you beyond belief.

> *My 68-day challenge was to be a non-smoker. I have smoked since age 14 (21 years). When people would find out that I smoked they couldn't believe it. My five kids had no idea that I was a smoker because I was ashamed to tell them. It didn't fit me but I kept doing it. When the 68-Day Challenge rolled out, I had been wishing for years that I had power over my addiction. I know how I became a non-smoker… I made a decision to be a non-smoker. It sounds simple, but that's what it boils down to. I also learned an even greater lesson as a leader: Provide an opportunity for your team to become better and some will. Invite your team to make a*

*decision for personal growth and some will. I have been a non-smoker for more than two months now and it feels great. I have energy that I haven't known in years and I feel a renewed sense of confidence and momentum. Thank you for creating the 68-Day Challenge.*

**Harley Blackburn**, sales manager—Grand Rapids

*I worked through all 7 phases of the 68 Day Challenge and it has had a profound impact on my life.*

*Through the process, I targeted "Health" as my FOCUS area, and in Phase 3 put together a plan with three steps to positively impact my life:*

*Exercise four times a week.*

*Take vitamins every day.*

*Adopt the personal affirmation: "I am a person who doesn't eat sugar.*

*In Phase 2 created a SMART goal: "I will lose 20 pounds by the end of the 68-Day Challenge, reaching my mid-point weight." You see, this is the first of several measured challenges for 2013.*

*In Phase 2, I also discovered Tim Ferris, and that discovery lead to the "Lift" app, which I now use and have shared both through LinkedIn and on the Art Van 68-Day Challenge Facebook page. It tracks my habits each day and provides positive reinforcement and tangible accountability as I complete the steps in my plan to achieve my goal.*

*In Phase 4 I found an accountability buddy and also interacted with the Facebook 68-Day Challenge group. I enjoyed being able to give support to others and also seeing their excitement as they progressed* through the challenge. I am still posting to the site as I continue my own personal challenge.

In Phase 5 I adapted and affirmed that keeping to my schedule was key to success. Phases 6 and 7 were overshadowed by some unexpected consequences of the Challenge. As I grew more in tune with my health I found myself more committed to maintaining it. I scheduled long-neglected dentist visits and also a few other tests, one of which found that I had severe sleep apnea. In fact, my resting blood oxygen level was 77% during the test. Thanks to the Challenge I now faithfully use a breathing machine at night.

Other unexpected health issues arose during the Challenge, and instead of putting off a doctor visit, as I would have done in the past, I consulted with my doctor. Although a few more tests are yet to be made, if there is a serious concern, we have found it early enough that it should respond to treatment.

Did I meet my goal? No, not as stated. I did lose 16 of the 20 pounds in my SMART goal. So, strictly speaking, I failed to meet the goal.

Have I impacted my health? Yes. My body now is getting the oxygen it needs, and my heart is not under the strain it felt from lack of oxygen and toting the 16 pounds!

There are other less quantifiable benefits: I am more connected to my co-workers, I took some risks in sharing on Facebook and maintaining accountability during the Challenge. I have recognized that I value myself and my health instead of ignoring issues and concerns. I have a few more doctor visits to conquer. I've started my next 68-Day Challenge with my focus on losing another ten pounds by May 15.

I've found I'm just a bit braver than I thought I was.

**Judey Kalchik**, store communications specialist

*Though my 68-Day Challenge is not the stuff of which books are made, I still wanted to share a smile with you. I went to my doctor on Monday and weighed in 31 pounds lighter! She commented on how great my blood work was and asked how I was doing this after all these years. I said, "Leaders lead. I so want to grow and be a better leader, and, in order to encourage buy-in for work-related initiatives, I have to show my team the initiatives work!" Now my challenge continues, and I am piggybacking with more movement and walking. Of course, I am slow, but I will gain momentum each day. We are never too old to change behaviors and do good things for ourselves that will spread. I am proof of that. Now this is a secret, I will be 60 in August so I have another reason to stay focused and on task. They say 60 is the new 40, and I want to be fabulous. You might say, I am PUMPED!*

*I cannot wait to read and hear of the great successes others are having. Focus is the tough part because I want to have a zillion new challenges going all at once. I get excited and think, "Now I can do this, or that, or another thing, too."*

*Make yours an extraordinary day!*

**Mary Clark**, store office manager—Bay City

GARY,
I AM SO
LOOKING
FORWARD
TO WORKING
WITH YOU
Ken Bussey

*My challenge was chosen for me, I didn't choose it. On the early evening of December 10th, I was working on setting up the Christmas lights on the front of my house. I walked out the front door to check to see if the timers were working and hit an iced-over front step, my leg buckling under me. My ankle swelled to twice its size within 10 minutes. Still, I was hoping that it was just a bad sprain, so I iced it and elevated it until the next morning. I walked under my own power into the urgent care center close to my house to have an X-ray, and found out that I had broken my ankle in two places! I saw an orthopedic specialist that afternoon who proceeded to put a hard cast on my right leg, up to the knee.*

*Immediately everything became harder to accomplish as for the first time in my 60 years of life, I became handicapped. Getting dressed, taking a shower, going to the bathroom, going from downstairs to upstairs, and getting from point A to point B all became daunting tasks. I had to rely on support at home and at work to assist me. I couldn't drive, so my wife became my mode of transportation. I relied on a friend at work to take me home some nights. Then there was the unforeseen pain, as my foot and ankle were swelling inside the hard cast, and, if I did too much or did not elevate it, it became painful.*

*Daunting and challenging are two words I now know well. As an officer of the company, it was my responsibility to recover as quickly as possible and that meant listening to the doctors and going to rehab as prescribed, not overdoing it, using my crutches, and keeping weight off of my ankle 100% of the time to quicken recovery. At three weeks, my doctor cut off my hard cast and took another X-ray of my ankle. It was healing, but he wanted to put another hard cast on my leg. I lobbied for a walking boot and he agreed, but only if I promised not to walk and to continue to use my crutches. I did exactly that and three weeks later, the bones had healed, but then came the next step: continue to use the walking boot and schedule rehab with physical therapy sessions. I have gone to every scheduled session and I am happy to report that today, less than 10 weeks later, I am about 90% recovered. I still have swelling and minor pain, but I am walking without a boot. It has taught me a valuable lesson: Never take your health and wellbeing for granted. If something happens, rely on your support team to help you through it and listen to everything the doctors tell you to do.*

**Ken Bussell**, vice president, financial services

The 68-Day Challenge is not just about health goals and new positive habits. The moving story you are about to read shows just how dramatic the results can be when you set your mind to changing your life. This associate really had to dig deep and make some major changes in her life. For those of us whose goals are simpler, such as quitting Diet Pepsi or exercising every day, the following letter should convince us that nothing is impossible.

*My 68-Day Challenge goal was very, very personal. I have wrestled with sending my story in—but in the end, I hope that if even one person reads this maybe they will be inspired to change their life, too.*

*Married for 23 years to a controlling and abusive husband, I knew I needed to make some changes, but the climb seemed much too high—we had a family business and three sons, so much invested, and seemingly so much to lose—and so I continued to lower my expectations and struggle through my days with the fake smile I had mastered many, many years earlier.*

*Stifled in our family business for 21 years, I took a huge leap and began interviewing for a new career last fall. It was liberating and terrifying all at the same time. I found a real home at this position at Art Van. My first day was December 3rd, 2012, but it was so much more than that. I really felt like I took the first important step to changing my life. Then one day, in my first few weeks, I received an email about a 68-day "change yourself, change your life" challenge. I decided this was the push that I needed.*

*The nine weeks that followed were a whirlwind.*

*Week #1: I researched attorneys and hired the best.*

*Week #2: I sat my boys down (23, 20 and 15) and explained to them what was about to happen— definitely my toughest day of the 68.*

*Week #3: With my ducks in a row and a lump in my throat, I told my husband.*

*Week #4: I filed for divorce.*

*Week #5: I hired a realtor to sell our home—it sold in eight days and for our asking price. Clearly, someone was looking out for me.*

*Week #6: I bought a beautiful new condo in a perfect spot [that had] the Macomb-Orchard bike trail running through the backyard.*

*Week #7: I closed on the condo. Art Van delivered a whole house of beautiful new furniture.*

*Week #8: With my older boys away at college, my youngest son and I moved into our new home. I slept soundly through the night for the first time in years, feeling safe. I woke up the next day, feeling happy, empowered, and in control of my future for the first time in two decades.*

*Week #9: My son turned to me one night during dinner and told me how glad he was that "we are so happy now." It made every second of the two months of back breaking work and rivers of tears worth it.*

*Everyone has SOMETHING they want or need to do to change their life. For some, it is as simple as working in a brisk walk once a day or stopping the munching between meals. For some, the obstacles and goals are bigger. Mine was huge. Would I have eventually gotten to the same place without the 68-Day Challenge? Probably, someday. Maybe. But it was the catalyst I needed, and I am grateful.*

*As far as what's the next challenge for me, I am not sure. I do know that, for right now, every day is about finding the good and being happy.*

*Thank you so much for the push.*

**Julie Kennedy**, advertising manager, print production

Okay, once again, are you ready to unleash your I-Pump? Now let's get into the 68 lessons of *Internal Pumptitude*.

# 1) Reinvent or become obsolete—compete with yourself

In *Pumptitude* (Chapter 11, #65), we clearly described how to start each year or each challenge with a clear vision and mission of what you want to achieve. You can go back to that book for a refresher. Here, I'm going to share another very interesting concept that I've used for developing strategic business plans and changing businesses for the better over the past several years.

Here's how it works: Imagine a fierce competitor coming to your city and to your market, and opening a retail store right beside yours. Envision that their team, their products, their service, their marketing and their brand are so strong that they will put your own business model at extreme risk.

What I do next makes this exercise extremely powerful. Once I've envisioned this awesome new hypothetical competitor and all of its threatening strengths, I work hard towards changing my current business model to look exactly like the imaginary business I so terribly feared. By doing this, year after year, I've been able to keep my business strategies relevant and in a continual state of reinvention.

You can also apply this imaginary concept at a personal level. Picture yourself as an employee whose boss is looking around for someone who could ultimately do a better job than you. Or he or she is looking for someone to promote into a newly elevated position. Imagine what this new employee would look like, such as his or her skills, education, experience, drive, ambition, personal brand, and overall attractiveness. Guess what? Whatever qualities you envision this highly desirable person to have, your immediate goal is to reinvent yourself into this person.

For me to grow as a top-performing CEO, I have to constantly play the "what if?" game. Is there another CEO the chairman and the board could be looking at that could be better, faster or stronger? I must clearly imagine this CEO competitor and reinvent myself into that person.

To apply this concept to your 68-Day Challenge, your goal is to be constantly growing, constantly changing, and constantly working towards making yourself so much better. You don't want to be an employee who worked for a company 30 years, the same year 30 times. Each year must be new and exciting. Each year you must be bringing something new to your job. Each year you must grow and evolve to the next level. Your goal is to have each year be a masterpiece on its own. Your objective throughout your life is to stay *relevant* and not become a *relic*, or worse, *obsolete*. This may seem a little harsh, but I challenge you to reinvent yourself or die trying.

## 2) One word

Reflecting back on *Pumptitude*, we described how important it is to develop your personal brand, your personal vision and your personal mission. If you recall, we challenged you to come up with one word at the beginning of each year that you could own, something that would describe everything you want to become.

Within seconds after being asked what should be my word, my wife Donna came up with the word "relentless."

In their book *One Word That Will Change Your Life*, co-authors John Gordon, Dan Britton and Jimmy Page explore the concept of developing and selecting one word that you embrace each year.

They share their three-step process for finding your one word:

1. Prepare your heart—eliminate noise and clutter, and free your mind to be open to new ideas.

2. Discover your word—ask simple questions of yourself to guide you to come up with your one word.

3. Live your word—have fun applying the word in every part of your life.

This easy-to-read book presents an incredibly powerful method for simplifying your business plan and your personal development strategy into one word. The book takes you through the process of creating your word and bringing it to life throughout the year. One way is to post the word on everything you see and touch as a constant reminder of the message.

The one word is a great addition to your 68-Day Challenge and can be worked into Phase 1 and Phase 2 on your personal worksheet. In selecting your one word, remember to include spiritual, physical, mental and emotional connections. This will ensure that your one word is absolutely the right one for you.

If I was to choose a favorite word to replace relentless, it would be *industrious*. I believe it truly describes the one percenters whose stories you will be reading in this book. Readers' Digest dictionary defines industrious as: showing assiduity in work or effort, hardworking, diligent, skillful, clever, busy.

Mike Lipkin suggests that the one word for many of us should be *grow*—to grow in every aspect of our lives. He especially likes this word because it puts no limits on your possibilities. Considering we are in a no-growth economy and environment, it is good to zig when the rest of the world is zagging.

Two other words that Mike promotes are *inspire* and *more*. You will read more about Mike's words in Chapter 8, #41 about the power of inspiration.

I have tried to integrate these three powerful words into everything I do. I crave to be inspired and to inspire others, and I believe that my relentless growth stems from my ability to integrate multiple activities in pursuit of that growth—personally and professionally. I'm always working on myself and our multiple businesses, so that they can become much more than they are today. I encourage you to apply one or all three of these words into your own future.

Before we move on, be reminded that the words we use shape our thoughts and our minds and then become our behavior and our outcomes. We become what we speak. We are the words we embrace.

## 3) Simple plan—less is more

Phase 3 of the 68-Day Challenge, *Write Your Plan*, is a critical part of your success. Developing your personal and professional plan and incorporating it into the 68-Day Challenge is an essential tool. Without a new plan each year, you have the likelihood of repeatedly covering old territory and perpetuating the same old, same old. The yearly plan ensures that you focus on new territory.

Did you know that when it comes to annual plans of any type, business or personal, 50 percent fall off after the end of January? That percentage increases to 75 percent not being followed by the end of February. This is primarily due to most plans' complexity and the amount of information included. People don't remember line graphs or financial charts. What we need to focus on is the simplicity of the plan. *Less is more.*

To help with your planning, I suggest you review Chapter 6, #35 of *Pumptitude*, where we covered setting smart goals along with Brian Tracy's seven steps to goal setting.

## 4) Ask yourself why

Why do you need to change? Why do you need to be in a constant state of improvement? Because at the end of the 68-Day Challenge, you don't want to find yourself looking back and feeling terrible that you didn't do anything or put any effort into the past 68 days. If you recall in *Maximum Pumptitude* (Chapter 10, #60), we described the definition of hell as looking back on your life and being terrified that you never became the person you could have been.

Now is the time to become the person you want to be so you can look back in pleasure, not pain. Heaven is having no regrets. If you neglect to make the changes to develop new habits and push yourself to new levels, you will find that 68 days goes by quickly, and, at the end of it all, you will be left with tremendous regret.

I don't want that to happen to you, so I'm going to share a secret. If you get to the end of the 68 days and you feel those regrets, guess what? You can start the challenge right over again. Right then. Don't be paralyzed because you didn't get anything done. Do it now. Yes, get on with it. You'll be better for it. *I guarantee it!*

## 5) Reinventing your personal brand

I came across a terrific article by Dorie Clark in *Harvard Business Review*, called "Reinventing your personal brand: How to change your image and create exciting new opportunities." The following five key learning points are sure to assist you with your 68-Day Challenge and your never-ending quest to be the best you can.

1. **Define your destination:** As a leader, if you want to change your course and expect people to follow you, you had better be sold on the idea yourself. The only way to do that is by practicing until the new you is second nature. Confidence is only going to come through preparedness. I did this when I decided to stretch myself by improving as a speaker. I sought out a new CEO coach who would push me to become a better speaker. After watching Mike Lipkin speak to my executive team, I knew I needed to infuse my speaking with new energy, new directives, and a new pressure to perform. One way to ignite that passion was to step into a journey that would push me to higher expectations of myself, mirroring someone who truly pushed me to excel in an area I had not yet conquered. When I made the move to my new coach, I began to see myself as that speaker, able to engage the room no matter who was in the audience. The transition into that new me was happening. Did it happen by circumstance? No. There were months of coaching, studying other speakers, reading, writing and practicing. As I began delivering more speeches, I saw that my rebranding had worked, as I started getting feedback like this:

   *I thought that Kim Yost was the best [ICSC] Idea Exchange keynote speaker we have ever had. He was meaningful and relevant and had important messages that worked for Art Van and can work for anyone if they are focused and work with a passion for the grind!*—Paul Magy, Esq., Clark Hill PLC.

Hearing comments like this, I felt a great sense of pride in knowing that all the hard work paid off. I had set my destination and made up my mind that I could and would do a great job.

2. **Leverage your points of difference:** Uniqueness is an obvious necessity if you want to stand out when rebranding yourself. You must pay attention to your effect on others to recognize what about you is engaging those around you and then work very hard on making those vital unique traits part of your reinvention. My CEO coach Mike Lipkin is from South Africa. His accent, coupled with the energetic delivery of truly profound messages, makes Mike stand out in the sea of motivational speakers. Once you have heard him, seen him, and enjoyed the strength of his messages, he is impossible to forget.

3. **Develop a narrative:** The story you tell yourself and others about your reinvention should reflect how the value of your past is contributing to the successes of your future. You are building on your past, not tearing it down. You do not want to have your hard work viewed as a sellout or a directional change because the old you was somehow wrong. Anything you are setting yourself up to be should be shared as an enhancement to the previous you. Make sure you tell this story well.

4. **Reintroduce yourself:** When you step out to sell the new you, those who have known you the longest will be the hardest to convince of your new skill set. These people see you as you used to see yourself. Remember that they are more concerned about their own world than yours. Eliminate any mixed messages and be consistent by only presenting the new you. Everything must reflect your rebrand. Be out there promoting your efforts the best you can. Hit it hard, because repetition is essential. Make sure your new skill set is up front and center and **be that change**.

5. **Prove your worth:** The proof is in the pudding. Work your new skills every chance you get and make sure what you are offering is of value! Make a difference and be compelling. I always follow what compels me; messages and people can sway me their way by giving me something that I feel I cannot live without, even if it is something small. You need to share consistently and creatively for certain, but if you also make it meaningful, you will not be forgotten.

Reinventing yourself should be fun. You should love who you want to be and enjoy getting there. Watch what happens around you, and it will help you see your way. The reactions on people's faces when you share will give you everything you need to hone your skills. Listen to feedback and give it the attention it deserves. Stick to your definite path of what you are trying to achieve and you will get definite results.

So with our 68-Day Challenge behind us and with many great ideas about reinventing ourselves, let's move onto how we can master success in everything we want to do.

## Art Van One Percenter: Michelle Dolski, Director, Organizational Development

Well, here we are at the introduction of our first one percenter and high achiever. When I joined Art Van in the fall of 2009, I had the fortunate opportunity to start working with Michelle and developing some exciting new programs in both sales and executive leadership. Michelle has not only inspired and motivated the Art Van team, she's done a lot of work on me. Get ready to enjoy her story.

||||||||||||||||||||||||||||||||||||||||||||||||||||||||||||||||||||||||||||||||||||||||||||||||||||

Michelle Dolski's 13 years in human resources started with Scott Shuptrine Interiors and then Frank's Nursery & Crafts. She rejoined the Art Van Furniture "family" in 2005 with a mission to create the ULTIMATE retail workforce. Working with key leaders and top performers, she has designed industry-leading education in sales, mattresses, delivery and leadership. These programs will be instrumental to improving talent inside Art Van as well as recruiting and building high-performing teams within new markets.

||||||||||||||||||||||||||||||||||||||||||||||||||||||||||||||||||||||||||||||||||||||||||||||||||||

## The power of choice

*Everything can be taken from a man*
*but one thing: the last of the human*
*freedoms—to choose one's attitude in*
*any given set of circumstances,*
*to choose one's own way.*
*—Viktor_E_Frankl*

In the book *Man's Search for Meaning*, Dr. Frankl describes laboring in four different Nazi death camps, including Auschwitz, while his parents, brother, and pregnant wife were brutally murdered. Even in the misery and brutality of a concentration camp, he was able to exercise the most important freedom of all—the freedom to choose your own attitude and spiritual well-being.

My personal and professional success was born from this very same concept. No matter what is going on around me, I happen to make better choices over bad ones every single day. While not ground breaking, it's not easy. It takes awareness, discipline, accountability, patience, and, most importantly, choosing to do the right thing even over your own self-interest.

## The 68-Day Challenge

True examples of the power of choice were the participants of the 68-Day Challenge. As you read in this chapter, this initiative had no strings attached and provided a process, as well as a support system, for anyone inside Art Van that wanted to jumpstart their 2013. The best part was that this was not a program created by Human Resources that had to be sold to the CEO. It was all Kim, pushing and inspiring us to get it started.

As I look back, what was the biggest difference between those who participated and those who didn't? Was it age? Nope. Was it status? Nope. Was it gender? Nope. It was that they made the choice to better themselves.

Do you want to unleash your own internal pumptitude? My advice is this:

## Start by first paying attention to your choices.

## Art Van One Percenter: David Van Elslander, Vice President, Merchandising

As the youngest son of the founder and chairman of Art Van Furniture, David Van has been a big contributor to the success of the company in several areas. He brings a passion and a focus each and every day that is beyond the norm. He lives with style and a commitment to excellence that makes him the one percenter he is. I'm so pleased to not only call him a colleague, but a dear friend. Enjoy the 68-Day Challenge through his eyes.

||||||||||||||||||||||||||||||||||||||||||||||||||||||||||||||||||||||||||||||||||||||

David, youngest son of Founder and Chairman Art Van Elslander, was raised in the business. Holding various positions in the Art Van organization, David found his passion in merchandising in 1990 and has been developing that passion for the past 23 years. David held positions in merchandising at Scott Shuptrine Furniture from 1990–2001, then did a brief stint at Rowe Furniture as business development manager before rejoining the family business in November 2005. David is currently responsible for merchandising for the clearance centers at Art Van and Art Van Pure Sleep.

||||||||||||||||||||||||||||||||||||||||||||||||||||||||||||||||||||||||||||||||||||||

## What happened to the relentless me?

I was honored when Mr. Yost asked if I would participate in his third book about I-Pump. After all, it was Kim who inspired me to take a look at how I was approaching each day and how I could make each one better. That's right, MAKING days great is up to the individual. It's all in how you prepare for and approach each day. So I decided to adopt a word for myself, one that I had when I was active in sports, one that kept me driven and one that describes me best. I have to admit I can become a bit annoying to some, but nevertheless, when I want something, I mean really, really, really want it badly, I am **relentless**.

## 2013: The 68-Day Challenge

At the beginning of 2013, Kim came up with a challenge to all of the employees at AVF. He called it the "68-Day Challenge." Participation was voluntary. The idea was to jump start the new year. Now, I had been claiming that I wanted to lose weight and had been making excuses for the past few years as to why I couldn't exercise. They were pretty common but weak excuses, "not enough time," "not a morning person," "too tired after work." I knew I needed to change my approach, so I accepted the Challenge. It was quite simple. I set the goal of how much I wanted to weigh, and I began running each morning. I ran as far I could, five days a week. I started at about three miles and am currently up to five miles (in the same amount of time). But here is the best part: not only did I lose the weight I wanted to, I have more energy, more focus, and more motivation than I have had in several years. It has made a big difference in every facet my life, professionally, personally and spiritually.

So if you're like I was, waiting for something to happen that moves you, stop waiting and start acting. Remember, YOU are the only person who can change YOU. Set a simple plan and act on it. Whether it's losing weight, learning a new skill, or growing in your personal, professional or spiritual relationships, YOU have the power inside of you. YOU can start MAKING every day a GREAT DAY. **What are you waiting for?**

# INTERNAL PUMPTITUDE

## — Chapter 2 —

# SAY YES, YOU CAN

*Belief comes first, expression comes second.—CEO coach Mike Lipkin*

This book is all about how to find internal pumptitude—how to fire up your motivation from the inside, so it can't be doused by anyone or anything. Internal definition overcomes external obstacles. True fulfillment begins with identifying ourselves as someone who can make things happen. We need to see ourselves as being destined for success. The next step is to declare our beliefs to the world so others become allies and supporters.

## 6) Ordinary people can do extraordinary things—you can overcome any odds

Here's a story that illustrates how the most ordinary of people can do the most extraordinary things. Now for years, I was a self-proclaimed non-golfer. I did everything in my power to get out of playing golf, whether it was for business or pleasure. But last year, I realized that spending time with my wife Donna and several of our key executives from Art Van on a golf course would be beneficial on many fronts.

Mid-summer last year, on a Sunday morning, Donna and I were golfing with Bob Price and Steve Glucksman, two of our vice-presidents. We were at the third hole, and, as soon as I hit the ball, Donna remarked that it was one of my best shots ever.

However, because the hole was up on a hill, we couldn't see the bottom of the pin from where we were standing. The three of them went up to the hole, searching not only for their own balls, but mine as well. Never dreaming that a guy who uses a driver for par three would ever hit a hole-in-one, they searched and searched for my ball, only to find that *it was inside the cup*!

I couldn't believe their response—they were far more excited than I was. Bob Price has been golfing for over 45 years, has never had a hole-in-one, or seen anyone get a hole-in-one. This was, in short, amazing.

If the story ended there, I probably wouldn't be telling it to you now, but it didn't. Three weeks later, on a different par three, this ridiculous and extraordinary accomplishment was achieved a second time. This miracle was witnessed by Donna and our vice president of human resources, Mr. Gary Duncan.

As I approached my drive for what would be my second hole-in-one, Mr. Duncan reminded me that my first hole-in-one was the biggest fluke he had ever heard of, and it would be impossible for me to ever repeat it again. I said, "Mr. Duncan, you just have to believe. And if you believe strong enough, it could just happen." I went onto the tee box, hit the ball, and voilà—my second hole-in-one in three weeks.

I've since learned that the odds of hitting two holes-in-one within three weeks are 20

million to one and that several golfers on the PGA tournament have *never* achieved a hole-in-one. So keep the faith, you golfers, and, for everyone else, remember that ordinary people can do extraordinary things.

## Now, you will not believe this!

I did not want to change the section that you just read, but had to add this exciting news bulletin. This morning, being Sunday, I was out golfing with Donna and two of our vice presidents, Mr. Bob Price and Mr. Gary Duncan. During this morning's golf game, lightning struck a third time. Yes, it was my third hole-in-one.

Norman Manley of California holds the record for most holes-in-one—59. Manley shot his first hole in one in 1964 and aced four holes in 1979. That's not too bad considering the odds of hitting a hole in one are roughly one in 40,000. I have come to realize the sheer odds against having one hole-in-one, let alone two. It seems every time I'm out socially and the subject of golf comes

up, very few people have seen or managed a hole-in-one. Now the impossible has been achieved a third time!

It happened on the eighth hole, and I went crazy and almost overdosed on mental endorphins. My first two holes-in-one were exciting, but this one was beyond belief. I think the odds of getting three holes-in-one in less than 12 months is in the trillions.

What also makes this hole-in-one so memorable is that Bob Price was there last summer for the first one, and Gary Duncan was there to witness the second one. Of course, Donna was there for both. Now all three of them were there to witness it again. Isn't this unimaginable? Why me? I'm not even a golfer! I use two clubs to do everything, a #5 rescue, and a #1 driver. My #5 rescue, I chip with it, I sand wedge with it, I putt with it. Two clubs. So to all you golfers, I can't believe it, either!

Getting a hole-in-one is like winning the lottery—the odds are massively against you, but thousands of people win the lottery every week. If you believe in luck, and you're willing to get on the course, you stand a chance. Take it.

## 7) Success is a choice

Whenever I start a presentation, I always ask three key questions. Regardless of who is in the audience, they always unanimously answer with an enthusiastic, "Yes!" Question #1 is: "How many of us believe that we can work harder on ourselves than we are currently doing?" Question #2 is: "How many of us believe that we can have a much stronger personal and professional plan for this year?" Question #3 is: "How many of us believe that if we work harder on ourselves and we work harder on our plan, we can ultimately create a much better year than we're on course to have at this point?"

The goal for all of us is to realize that we can always constantly increase our effort in everything we do. No matter how confident you are that you've been working on yourself and that you have a solid plan, we can all do better. We can make a conscious choice as to how much effort we're prepared to put into our success and then dial it up!

Here are some of the success behaviors that I am constantly working on that I believe will help you in your own efforts for greater success:

- live in constant stretch
- always push the boundaries
- say no to cruise control or auto-pilot
- sweat the small stuff, sweat the big stuff, go the extra mile
- put your heart and soul into everything you do
- have excellence as part of your personal brand

## 8) Lifetime of successful behavior and I-Accountability

There are compounding benefits of doing small things consistently. A good example is the 23-hour day (*Pumptitude*, Chapter 7; Chapter 5, #23 in this book), where you exercise relentlessly every day for one hour to maximize your return on the remaining 23 hours. I work out first thing every morning and I've done this for 35 years.

A successful life comes from a lifetime of successful behavior. Every day is your life in miniature, a microcosm. Every day could be THE day. If we make every day count, they will add up to a great life.

As much as it's important to have I-Pump, it's important to have I-Accountability. In their book *The Oz Principle: Getting Results Through Individual And Organizational Accountability*, Roger Connors, Tom Smith and Craig Hickman share that we have become a nation of finger pointers, complainers, and people who believe we are victims. This is not for us. Our future is in our own control and definitely not left up to others.

The authors use the well-loved story *The Wizard of Oz* to illustrate their solution. In the story, Dorothy, Scarecrow, Tin Man and the Cowardly Lion were all searching for something they felt was missing. Yet, when they finally meet the Wizard of Oz, he showed them and *convinced* them that they had those things within them all along.

What we learn from *The Wizard of Oz* and so many other examples in life is that **if it's going to be, it's up to me** and not someone else. We have to be accountable, each and every day, for building a high-achieving life. It is this personal accountability that drives all one percenters. We don't look to blame others for our lot in life. We look inward, not outward, for our results. In *Maximum Pumptitude*, Chapter 5, #30, I warned you to avoid death by entitlement. Looking for entitlement will be the road to our doom. If you ever need a reminder of who you need to be counting on, head for the nearest mirror.

We can take away these key points from *The Oz Principle*:

1. In life you are either living above or below a certain line of personal accountability. When you live below the line, it's about feeling like a victim, blaming others, and feeling out of control. **Live above the line**, control your destiny, and blame no one.

2. Your powerful personal accountability can have a positive reflection on others, particularly if you're in a leadership role.

3. If you ever need a reminder, look to *The Wizard of Oz* (and your mirror) for great examples that that success starts first from within.

## 9) The you of today

The you of tomorrow is entirely dependent on the you of today. In Chapter 12 of *Pumptitude*, we asked you to imagine yourself in the future, taking the book off the shelf 10 years later, and seeing how many changes you'd put into place based on what you'd learned. As I stated previously, the things you do today have a compounding impact on the you you'll be tomorrow.

If you want to stay forever young, engage in activities that will make you healthy. Our faces and bodies are a record of how we have lived. A good life comes from a good lifestyle. Now is the time to create the future. How do you want to look when you're 80?

This is the ultimate wake-up call: When someone meets you 20 years from now, will they be impressed by how you've led your life? Would they see you as a role model? Or would they see you as a warning of what could happen?

## 10) Major in the majors

Many people put a lot of effort into their careers and their lives, yet, at the end of a year or even a few years, there really hasn't been any amazing outcome. The real clarity is to make sure you're not just spinning your wheels on minor things, but that you're accomplishing something that's measurable, results-oriented, and gives you the desired outcome.

I constantly remind my colleagues to major in the majors, not major in the minors. I will often use cash as a visible reminder of this concept, and you can do this too.

On your desk, lay out a series of coins. From right to left, place a penny, then a nickel, then a dime, then a quarter, then, finally, a silver dollar. The goal is to focus on the dollars, not the pennies. If you focus on pennies, you will achieve pennies. If you focus on nickels, you will achieve nickels. If you focus on dollars, you will ultimately achieve dollars. So constantly ask yourself, "What is the value of the prize I am working towards? Am I keeping my focus on the big picture, and am I working on the truly big results?"

Well, we have just concluded our second chapter. Let's read on about exciting one percenters and how you can find your own passion, your own methods of overachieving, and some interesting human drivers. Are you ready? Put on your seatbelt and let's go!

## One Percenter: Bob "Idea Man" Hooey, Creative Catalyst

Bob "Idea Man" Hooey has been a dear friend of mine for years. We have had countless professional and personal experiences that fill a big place in my Life Chest. He travels the world relentlessly with a passion to inspire. Enjoy his story of focus, creativity, and discipline.

‖‖‖‖‖‖‖‖‖‖‖‖‖‖‖‖‖‖‖‖‖‖‖‖‖‖‖‖‖‖‖‖‖‖‖‖‖‖‖‖‖‖‖‖‖‖‖‖‖‖‖‖‖‖‖‖‖‖‖‖‖‖

Bob Hooey is an award-winning speaker, author and leader who has garnered international recognition from his peers and clients. His innovative *Ideas At Work* are published globally in corporate, association, trade and consumer publications. His *ideas* have allowed him to visit 39 countries, so far. As he says, "Have mouth, will travel." His greatest passion is being able to encourage people to move out of their comfort zones into the winner's zone. He challenges them to choose success and become extraordinary in their lives and personal leadership.

‖‖‖‖‖‖‖‖‖‖‖‖‖‖‖‖‖‖‖‖‖‖‖‖‖‖‖‖‖‖‖‖‖‖‖‖‖‖‖‖‖‖‖‖‖‖‖‖‖‖‖‖‖‖‖‖‖‖‖‖‖‖

I am often asked how I was able to create the amazing wins in my life. I simply state, "If I can do it, so can you!" In truth, if you have the dreams and the *inner* desire, are willing to be disciplined, and focus your energies and mindset, you can easily surpass what I have done so far. **Big dreams coupled with strategic steps lead to significant success!**

I'm also asked how I keep positive and focused. On *home* days, I am awakened by our furry kids. I get up, feed them, do a few stretches, read something positive, and reflect on the game plan set the night before. I choose to write prior to digging into other projects, such as presentation prep for a client or one of my charity events. The 30+ books I have written were an act of desire and *discipline*. On *road* days, my routine is similar, but without the furry alarm clocks.

There are also days in which I need a nudge or boost. This is where I touch base with a select group of friends for encouragement, such as my cheerleader Kim (who continues to challenge me) or my wife Irene (who often quotes me to me). Then I dig back into my work.

My greatest joy is seeing my *Ideas At Work* within an organization and seeing people take personal leadership, play to their strengths, and thrive. I work diligently to create something significant that will enhance my *brand* and my ability to help people grow and win. I love what I do and plan on staying healthy to do it well into my 80s.

Success is a choice you make each day. Each day you can choose to create BIG dreams and focus on the strategic steps that will make them a vivid reality. Each decision acted upon helps to create a lifetime of success and significance. **Say YES, you can!**

## Art Van One Percenter: Ruth Sinawi, Sales Executive

As our second one percenter in the chapter "Say Yes, You Can," no one I've ever met is better suited to this chapter. She is an individual who has set a bar in high achievement in sales and in life that is difficult for any of us to meet. The one remarkable quality of Ruth Sinawi is that she will stop at any time to help a sales colleague become better at what they do by sharing her disciplines and proven methods. Both Donna and I have become great spectators and fans of Ruth's never-ending achievements. Enjoy her story, knowing clearly that she is a big reason why Art Van enjoys the success that it does today.

||||||||||||||||||||||||||||||||||||||||||||||||||||||||||||||||||||||||||||||||||||||||||||||||||||||||||||||

Ruth Sinawi joined Art Van Furniture in 1992 and has worked at the Novi, MI, store for her entire career. Ruth has accumulated staggering sales numbers, including 19 consecutive years as a member of the Art Van **Chairman's Circle** (minimum $1,350,000 in sales per calendar year). In 2012, Ruth had a record high $1,984,000 in delivered sales, which is the all-time highest in one year at Art Van Furniture. Growing up in a family that taught her to have a tireless work ethic, she has made her family proud with her relentless pursuit of continued achievement. Her success has helped Ruth provide for her loving family, including five children and four grandchildren.

||||||||||||||||||||||||||||||||||||||||||||||||||||||||||||||||||||||||||||||||||||||||||||||||||||||||||||||

## What is the secret to my success?

There are several things that have helped make me as successful as I have been over the years, with one being just as important as the next. I'm very passionate about working for Art Van Furniture, and I love what I do. This passion has allowed me to maintain a positive attitude and enthusiasm, which is extremely important to show my clients. If you don't show your guests, both internal and external, that you care about them, you have no chance at being successful! I treat my clients the same way I treat my family. I listen to what their needs are and take care of them from start to finish.

Communication is one of the most important skills to have when on the sales floor. If you're a good communicator and can truly listen and understand your clients and show them you care, there is a real good chance you will make the sale, time and time again. If people trust you, they will not only buy from you once, but they'll come back again and refer friends and family to you.

## Art Van Furniture is a family

Through it all, no matter how successful a year I have had, I remain humble. To me, you can't be a success unless you stay humble and show gratitude to everyone who has helped you along the way. Art Van Elslander believed in me from the very beginning and instilled the confidence in me that I need to succeed. His leadership has truly inspired me to do my best each and every day, and I owe most of my success to him and his family. Gary Van and David Van continue to build on this great family-run business. Art Van Elslander has also brought in some terrific leadership in CEO Kim Yost. Mr. Yost has provided a great atmosphere to work and to sell. Under Mr. Yost, I have posted record sales the last three years, and I owe him much of the credit because of the way he directs and leads. He puts people in positions to be successful and I am a direct reflection of that. I love to think I am an ambassador for Art Van Furniture. I'm proud to be a part of this wonderful company and look forward to many more future successes.

# INTERNAL PUMPTITUDE

# — Chapter 3 —

# ONE PERCENTERS

*Knowing is not enough; we must apply.*
*Willing is not enough; we must do.*
*—Johann Wolfgang von Goethe*

There is no accident in your success and achievements. When reading about and talking to hundreds of highly successful individuals, they all have one thing in common: they all discuss, ever so casually, their years of hard work and the countless hours that it took to achieve their goals and their lifelong dreams. Let there be no mistake. The one percenters of the population—those who make an amazing life and a legacy worth learning from—all put unimaginable effort into what they accomplish. As I've stated previously, "such is the effort, such is the reward." (*Pumptitude*, Chapter 1, #2.) And those rewards will dazzle you.

In this chapter, you will read several great stories and the teachings of some pretty terrific authors and public speakers. Are you ready?

## 11) Find your passion

Some time ago, I received an audiobook called *Finding Your Passion*, by an author and professional speaker named Cheryl Richardson. She shares several great things that can teach each and every one of us to not only find our passion, but sustain it. Remember, passion is not an external event. It is very personal and from within; it is the ultimate internal experience. Here are five gems I would like to pass on from Cheryl's teachings:

1. **Get to know yourself**. Get to know yourself by getting connected to your feelings so you can clearly understand what makes you feel good or bad. You need to take this time for yourself to discover what really fires you up. In *Pumptitude* (Chapter 1, #9), we talked about completing a 360-degree assessment and challenged you to determine where you are in all aspects of your life, versus where you want to be. Remember that Schmonday (*Pumptitude*, Chapter 3) is a great time to reconnect and discover exactly where to find your passion. The unfortunate situation for many of us is that we don't find this passion in our current jobs. Our hobbies, fitness activities, and time spent with friends and family contribute far more to our passion than the careers we've selected. Sadly, too many of us finish school, take our first jobs, and end up being at the same place for too long, even if we're not passionate about that work. What Cheryl talks about is actually taking the time to try many different careers, jobs and experiences, before we settle on the career that we will spend years at. I can tell you that I am blessed by having a career like no other. My passion is in selling and building people and companies, and there isn't a single day that goes by that I'm not doing what I'm clearly passionate about. This is the wish that both Cheryl and I share for each of you.

2. **Taking things away**. Finding your passion is not always about adding things to your life, like new cars, new jobs, new friends, or even new furniture. To find your passion, it can be just as important to take things out of your life, for example, the people who are adding negativity to your life, the amount of complexity and activities that you put into a given workweek, or habits and behaviors that are not positive and proactive. Taking things away, as opposed to always adding, is the key learning here.

3. **Our role models**. Our role models and the people we admire can lead us to discover our own passion and so can the people we envy. I always thought that my role models had to be the people I worked with or read about, but Cheryl taught me to expand my thinking and see the *good* side of envy. Envy can be a negative human feeling, but it can also be a great thing if it motivates you to take positive action. It needs to build you up, not tear you down. Envy needs to be admiration that inspires action to reach a similar state. Here are three of the people I envy and would like to be more like: **James Bond** because he drives fancy cars, travels to exotic places, has cool watches, always has amazing clothing, dines in the most spectacular restaurants, and he always gets the villains; **Marco Polo** because he ventured to places that had never before been seen by an Italian, sat beside the throne of Genghis Khan, brought back several wonders of the world from Asia (including the spaghetti noodle), ventured to places that many only dream about, and shared his findings and explorations with the world; and **Howard Hughes** because his passion for aviation was unequaled; he focused on inventing and re-inventing flight, produced some of the most amazing black and white movies, and put himself into his work as if his life depended on it (and in many cases, financially, it did, like when he was building the world's largest transport plane, the Spruce Goose). So when you look for your passion and benchmark yourself to others, as Cheryl says, look at who you envy and what they've done to find their passion and learn from that. This makes envy a very positive feeling.

4. **Resume, instead**. Sometimes you'll try, day after day, to find your passion at your job, and no matter how much effort you put into your job and into re-inventing yourself, you still come up short. What should you do then? Cheryl's advice is to stop looking for passion at your job and look for your resume instead.

5. **Face your fears**. Face your fears like they don't exist. What's the worst thing that will happen when you try? You will succeed! Remember, when you try something, you've already succeeded. Your attitude will give you altitude (*Pumptitude*, Chapter 2).

## 12) 10 steps to overachieving

In Rick Pitino's bestselling book, *Success is a Choice*, he details these 10 steps to overachieving in business and in life. Here are his 10 steps, along with my notes about each one. **You're going to love these!**

1. **Build self-esteem**: Self-esteem is vital to achieving. You must not only feel good about yourself, you must also feel you can perform and accomplish great things. You must believe that you deserve success. Self-esteem has to be earned to have significant value. You do have control over your life. Your success or failure is up to you.

2. **Set demanding goals**: Throughout the *Pumptitude* series, we have challenged you to be great goal setters (Brian Tracy's ideas in Chapter 6, #35 of *Pumptitude*, and earlier in this book in Chapter 1 about the 68-Day Challenge). The process of setting and achieving goals helps you understand the effort it takes to meet each one. Goal setting is a process of building blocks; one goal, once achieved, builds on another goal and so on and so on. The key is to keep creating demanding goals for yourself, goals that allow you to reach your full potential.

3. **Always be positive**: As we have indicated repeatedly, beginning in Chapter 2 of *Pumptitude*, attitude determines altitude. Positive people tend to find the good in everything. In the introduction to that chapter, we talked about Jon Gordon's book, *The Shark and the Goldfish*, and his simple premise that it's the positive fish who find more food. So the learning here is that attitude, and a positive one, is everything.

4. **Establish good habits**: This book is full of reminders that building on positive habits will give you compounding benefits. Developing these habits in everything you do will take your game to another level, both personally and professionally. I urge you to continue to build on the positive habits of daily reading, daily exercise, and your own weekly Schmonday.

5. **Master the art of communication**: Another habit that needs constant and never-ending improving is being a great communicator. If you recall in *Pumptitude* (Chapter 10, #53), we talked about John Maxwell's book, *Everyone Communicates, Few Connect: What the Most Effective People Do Differently*, and we encouraged you to become a great connector. You will find that everything you want to accomplish in life, particularly as a leader, mentor or parent, can all be done so much more successfully when you communicate well and, ultimately, when you connect. I am on a personal crusade to eliminate three words from the English language: um, ah, oo. Using these words can distract your listeners, make you seem unprepared, and impair your ability to connect with your audience. People may think you're using the words as fillers to allow yourself to catch up and engage your mind with the discussion you're having. So get those words out of your vocabulary, be clear and decisive when you communicate, and you will find that you'll have a much better chance of connecting.

6. **Learn from role models**: In *Maximum Pumptitude*, Chapter 11, #68, I described Stage 6 of life. That is the time to give back by sharing what you've learned and by becoming a coach and mentor to others. So isn't it so interesting that Rick's sixth step for achieving is to learn from role models? Learning from others can often help you make up your lack of experience, and, if these role models become ones that you envy (as we discussed above in Cheryl Richardson's work), they will challenge you to become someone you may never have known you could become.

7. **Thrive on pressure**: In Chapter 12, #65, you'll be reading about The One Percenters Course. We took the students of this course to a place they'd never been before. They were stressed out, full of anxiety, and some really let the pressure get to them, but when they completed their course, the sense of success was outstanding. This step is all about stress for success and pressing yourself to go beyond.

8. **Be ferociously persistent**: Anyone can be great and perform to the hilt for a day, a week, or a month, but if you want to be successful over the long haul, you must be willing to stay the course. This is where the combination of good habits, strong persistence, and creating a life that's a marathon, not a sprint, will pay off. Clearly, everything that we've been sharing with you in this *Pumptitude* series is about persistence and constant and never-ending improvement.

9. **Learn from adversity**: In *Maximum Pumptitude*, #12, "Ride out the cycle of self-improvement," we talk about how you never want to let a crisis go without building on that opportunity for success. As Mike Lipkin says, a crisis is a terrible thing to waste. When adversity hits, as you know it will, deal with it head on. You can't run from it, and you can't pretend it doesn't exist. You can't ignore it, or simply wait for it to go away. Use what you have read throughout these three books to prepare to deal with the adversity of life.

10. **Survive success**: There is no endpoint to your dream, and it's not enough to become successful. The trick is to become more successful every year by checking your ego at the door, staying smart, hungry and humble, developing an attitude of humility, and becoming a Level 5 leader (you'll learn how in Chapter 10, #49). How many times have we read or heard about successful people who fall prey to the dangers of bad habits and letting success go to their heads? This is not for you. As Rick tells us, success is great when managed and built upon.

# 13) 10 human drivers that will charge you up

The ideas behind these 10 human drivers from Brendon Burchard's *The Charge* are woven into my three books. Here are the drivers, with some Yost-isms tossed in for good measure.

1. **Control**: We all know when controlling something hinders and when it helps. We also may need to recognize when to relinquish control for the better good. This is especially important when working with teams. You need to let others share in the beauty of success and that may mean allowing someone else to take the reins if they are prepared to do so. Julie Donegan, Donna's associate at Life2000 (you'll read more about Donna and her team in Chapter 11), shares that when Donna asked her to pull together some ideas about the Life Chest brand and then left without giving any parameters or guidelines, Julie felt more empowered to really step up and be creative. The result was a winning new logo!

2. **Competence**: People who have not developed a high level of competence will usually only choose what is familiar and easy, as it takes less effort to accomplish what they already know. But this limits their experience in life and condemns them to a life of following rather than leading.

3. **Congruence**: If I expect more of myself and frame my day to stay true to those expectations, I will do whatever I can to achieve what I set out to do. In *The Charge*, Brendon Burchard suggests that you chose three words that define the way you think of yourself and three words that would define how you interact with others. He then suggests that you fashion your behaviors to stay congruent with these words.

4. **Caring**: When we talk about caring, I will bet that most people immediately think of what they have done for someone else. Burchard, like many leadership experts, encourages leaders to care for ourselves first, and not let busy schedules steer us into fast food restaurants or sleep-depriving travel arrangements.

5. **Connection**: Connection is how we create happier and deeper relationships. A lot of us are surrounded by people every day, some we will know peripherally and some we will know intimately. We sometimes spend more time with the first group than the second. It takes more effort to build on our intimate relationships, but they are the ones that really matter. *The Charge* suggests we work hard on cultivating our connections with our families and friends. As I have shared many times, this social capital is extremely important to your happiness and success.

6. **Change**: When you stay idle, life is boring, stale and dull. Change is like a shot of adrenaline. In the midst of change, you pay attention to everything around you as you feel the excitement that's driving the change. About trying new things, Julie Donegan says, "Don't betray your inner instincts but don't let yourself get in your way either. Confusing inhibition with intuition is one of the easiest ways to miss out on life."

7. **Challenge**: If you do not challenge yourself to stretch beyond everything you know, life becomes mundane. Being busy is challenging, but that alone isn't a fulfilling enough challenge. In *The Charge*, Brendon talks about focusing on the journey. This gives you more appreciation of your accomplishments and the challenges you've faced and overcome as you've stepped into a bolder, better side of life.

8. **Creative expression**: Creative expression is the most fun part of ourselves. We are all unique. Everything you do expresses something about you—how you speak, your way of dress, the car you drive, all of it. So don't just watch life pass by, participate! Decorate the world with your distinctive expressions—sing, dance, laugh, learn, and do it all with style.

9. **Contribution**: When you're playing tennis or golf, doesn't it feel better when you play full out and hold nothing back

even if you lose? That is what it means to contribute your all. Find a cause you are passionate about and go all in. Do meaningful things. Give it your proper attention and keep going! Help others learn, give them everything you can, share, share, share. Leave the world better than you found it.

10. **Consciousness**: Be aware of your thoughts. Do not be on auto pilot. What you are thinking is showing even if unspoken; it shows in your demeanor and attitude, so think wisely! Behave wisely as well. What you do says everything about who you are. Pay attention to others; see beyond their exterior and observe how they are feeling and responding to you. Use your strengths and these feelings will be more positive and powerful.

## 14) Dare to be one who is willing to pay the price

Several years ago, I attended a business seminar that was held during the difficult recession of the early 80s, and I learned a very interesting lesson. One of the session instructor's painted a mental picture for the audience that each of us owned a business that was about to go bankrupt. Millions of dollars would be lost, hundreds of jobs would be eliminated, and the lives of all the employees would take a dramatic change for the worst.

After we all had this mental picture of extreme disaster for each of our businesses, the instructor held up a silver cigar clipper. Now if you've never seen a cigar clipper, they have razor-sharp cutting edges, which squeeze together to cut the tip off a cigar. He said, "What if I told you that if I were to use this cigar clipper to cut a quarter-inch off the baby finger on your left hand, all the disaster pending for your business would be reversed and your business would enjoy unlimited success and ultimately survive the recession—who would let me clip their finger?" He asked for a show of hands from some 200 in attendance. Only three put up their hand. I was one of the three.

Did I really believe in his hypothetical scenario? Probably not, but what was amazing learning was that the room was filled with business owners, CEOs and presidents, representing hundreds of businesses, yet only a few were prepared to make a personal sacrifice to save those businesses. Now, I'm not suggesting that we should ever realize this degree of sacrifice when it comes to winning versus losing, particularly when it comes to saving your business, but the learning here is that it is the one percenters, the top graders, the executives that play all out and are fully in, who raise their hand and say, "Yes, I'll do it!"

## 15) Be relentless—find the treasure in the trash

In *Pumptitude*, I told you how my wife Donna came up with the one word that I could use as the basis for building my vision, mission and personal brand. That one word was *relentless*. Here's a fun story that ended up with a great result because of my being so relentless.

We were entertaining several of our friends in our wine cellar, on the night before Donna was traveling to the west coast. She had done a great job with another one of her amazing meals, having spent the day chopping, dicing and mixing her several courses. Unbeknownst to her, at some point during the day she had misplaced her wedding ring, only realizing it after all our company had left.

She looked for it but couldn't find it, and, with a cab coming to pick her up at 5:30 a.m. to take her to the airport, she finally just tried to go to sleep. All night she worried, where was her wedding ring? In the morning, she told me what had happened. I asked if she truly believed she hadn't misplaced it anywhere else but the kitchen; she said she was confident it was there somewhere.

We searched together for a while, but she had to get in the cab and go to the airport. After she left, I went out to the garage and pulled three large, fully-loaded garbage bags from our outside garbage bins. These three large garbage bags contained several plastic bags filled with food and leftovers, bits and pieces from the meal the night before. Now to hopefully give my wife peace of mind and a great ride on a five-hour flight west, I set upon going through the three garbage bags and all their contents, one by one.

I set up an assembly line in the kitchen, from literally one end to the other. I was almost to the bottom of the second garbage bag, having looked at every single item in those bags—yuck!—when I found my wife's wedding ring smushed into a tomato. With great glee and excitement, I phoned my wife as she was just about to board an airplane and told her I had found the ring in the tomato. Of course, she was relieved, as was I, and I took the opportunity to remind her that if I wasn't so relentless, her wedding ring would be in a landfill somewhere in southeast Michigan.

As a footnote, Donna's two-and-a-half carat wedding ring had a special meaning to me. I bought that diamond years before I met her, in Cape Town, South Africa, during a trip I took to the jungle. I spent almost my life savings on that diamond. God forbid that it would have ended up in a dumpster and ultimately in a landfill. I also had another reminder of how important it is to have faith and just "dive in."

## 16) If you want more, you must become more

In one of his many presentations to the Art Van team, Mike Lipkin spoke about the importance of becoming more. I've come to learn that the real power of the word *more* is not about accumulating more physical things, but it is about your personal development.

To maximize your personal development, you must want more and expect more, which will then ultimately allow you to **become more**. Here are some uses of the word *more* that can benefit us all in our careers and in our personal lives.

- We must learn more.

- We must see more.

- We must share more.

- We must read more.

- We must experience more.

- We must risk more.

- We must grow more.

- We must imagine more.

Looking closely at all successful companies, teams and people, the one common thread woven through all of them is an extraordinary work ethic. Your work ethic has to be second to none. You must hold nothing back, play full out every day; if anybody thinks otherwise, they're believing in magic.

Diane Charles, one of our leadership team members at Art Van, recently received a 25-year career award from the television and broadcasting industry. The award is called the Silver Circle, and it was given to her at a prestigious banquet amongst several of her peers and colleagues. At the conclusion of her acceptance speech, she read this "Welcome to Apple" note that struck her in a powerful way and, as she said, described her work in the industry so well:

> There is work and there is your life's work. The kind of work that has your fingerprints all over it. The kind of work that you never compromise on. That you'd sacrifice a weekend for. You can do that kind of work at Apple. People don't come here to play it safe. They come here to swim in the deep end. They want their work to add up to something. Something big. Something that couldn't happen anywhere else. Welcome to Apple.

At Art Van, we have worked hard for over five decades to become an organization where winners come to win. Over the last several years, I have enjoyed being surrounded with these amazing winners and sharing their stories with you in my books. Gary Duncan, our chief people officer, is committed to the highest level of employee engagement, as you'll discover at the end of Chapter 12. He regularly conducts one-hour lunch and learn sessions on self-development topics. One of his lunch and learns, which is very beneficial for all one percenters and high achievers, is True Colors. We spoke about True Colors in *Maximum Pumptitude*, Chapter 11, "The Six Stages of Life." The True Colors exercise involves answering several questions regarding your likes, dislikes, habits, and behaviors.

In order to become more, you need to clearly see who you are now. Your answers to the True Colors questions are used to profile you into one of four colors—blue, green, orange or gold. Depending on your color, the materials describe your personal strengths and passions in detail. This also helps you understand the other colors and the people to whom you are closest. I strongly recommend that whether you use True Colors or another method, you take the time to do a personality analysis to learn more about yourself and clearly understand your strengths. From all I have read and experienced, it is more important to focus on maximizing your strengths, than concentrating on your weaknesses. It is your strengths and doing outstanding things that will drive your career.

Now, for some of us, going through a personality analysis, particularly a 360-degree assessment that collects input from the people around us, leads to discovering fatal flaws in our behavior. These fatal flaws need to be eradicated as soon as we come to realize them—no matter how strong our strengths are and no matter how positive our contribution may be, fatal flaws will always wipe out our strengths. For example, if we have negative attitudes, if we're always a naysayer, and we don't support and work well with others, these negative behaviors will eclipse all our positive contributions.

Wow, wasn't that an amazing chapter, filled with great nuggets? I encourage you to mark up that chapter with highlighters and checkmarks. If you need extra motivation, pull the pages right out the book so you can stick them in front of you every day.

Now let's get on to Chapter 4, titled "No Fear." Stay with me because as we're progressing through these chapters, we're building a solid foundation for incredible success.

## Art Van One Percenter: Amelia Ellenstein, Vice President, Brand Strategy and Store Environment

What a treat to have Amelia contribute to I-Pump! This high-energy high achiever is what this book is all about. You will read that she has contributed to several great successes in Art Van's past, present, and future development. She brings her A game every day and motivates her team like a true one percenter. Enjoy her 10 essential behaviors for developing an amazing environment.

||||||||||||||||||||||||||||||||||||||||||||||||||||||||||||||||||||||||||||||||||||||||||||||||||||||

Amelia Ellenstein joined the management team at Art Van Furniture in February 2007. In 2011, her role was expanded to include all branding and in-store merchandising and she is now the VP of Brand Strategy and Store Environment. Amelia developed the company's first ever visual merchandising strategy, spearheaded the innovative PureSleep retail concept, and pioneered the Art Van Promise—the company's first formal brand point of view.

||||||||||||||||||||||||||||||||||||||||||||||||||||||||||||||||||||||||||||||||||||||||||||||||||||||

I didn't find my passion, it found me! It was November 1997, and I was working part time at The Gap as a sales associate during college. The holidays were approaching, and the visual merchandiser at our store had just quit.

In a panic, my store manager ran up to me, "Amelia, you're studying art, right?" I nodded yes. "Great, you're our new visual merchandiser!" Cautiously, I opened the door to the back room—the steamer was bubbling over, glitter coated the floor, and Christmas trees were tipped over like fallen timber. And so began my career as a visual merchandiser.

Who knew that I would turn a part-time job selling jeans into a rewarding career? When I consider my professional successes *and my failures*, I am able to pinpoint one consistent theme in my best work: collaboration. This is what creates a foundation for my most out-of-the-box, innovative work.

Here are 10 essential behaviors for developing collaborative environments that encourage imaginative people to practice their craft.

1. Find a way to say yes when you want to say no.

2. Hold on loosely. Focus on the end goal and let others contribute to that goal in their own way.

3. Recognize that good ideas come from everywhere.

4. You can argue or you can collaborate. One is a lot more productive than the other.

5. Remove the word "but"; replace it with "and."

6. Give others the benefit of the doubt—people are rarely malicious, often just poor communicators.

7. Everyone's perception of reality is different, and their reality is their normal.

8. Don't try to solve a problem via email—you'll end up with a bigger problem.

9. Ignore your mother's advice: Talk to strangers.

10. Learn to recognize your own "grumptitude." When you feel it coming on, take a break, ask for help, apologize.

## One Percenter: Florine Mark, President and CEO, The WW Group Inc.

Florine Mark has been an advisory board member of Art Van for the past few years. She challenges us and asks questions like no other member. Her drive and commitment to excellence is beyond belief. As a person who has battled diets and weight ever since playing hockey as a kid, I appreciate her story and I know you will as well.

||||||||||||||||||||||||||||||||||||||||||||||||||||||||||||||||||||||||||||||||||||||||||||||||||||||||

Florine Mark, president and CEO of The WW Group Inc., based in Farmington Hills, uses her knowledge, energy and experience as the leading U.S. franchise holder of Weight Watchers International to help people help themselves.

Today, in addition to her Weight Watchers franchises, she is a well-known radio and television personality in the Detroit area, and she is the author of *Talk to the Mirror*, a motivational, inspirational book that talks about how to have a healthier, happier life.

Community involvement is also very important to her, and she serves as an advisor, an advocate, and a board member on approximately 40 committees and civic organizations.

||||||||||||||||||||||||||||||||||||||||||||||||||||||||||||||||||||||||||||||||||||||||||||||||||||||||

I was a fat baby, who grew to be a fat child, who became a fat adult, but I thought about dieting my whole life. I lost 50 pounds nine different times… and then I landed in the hospital from a doctor-prescribed diet pill, known today as speed.

I'll be the first one to tell you, weight loss is an emotional battle as much as it is a health battle, and I'll bet that anyone who has fought with their weight knows this.

Everyone who works at Weight Watchers knows it. They have all had a weight problem, sat in the classes, lost the weight, and gone through maintenance, just like me. We know first-hand the emotional highs and lows of weight loss because we've had to lose the weight. We connect with our members because we are not just Weight Watchers employees, we are members, we are role models, and we are always working—every day—to keep the weight off and stay healthy.

Healthy living allows me to volunteer, which is also important to me. I am able to donate my time, my knowledge and my resources, while still handling my other daily responsibilities because my healthy lifestyle fills me with an abundance of energy and a lot of gratitude for what I have. Volunteering is how I show my appreciation, because I believe that those who can afford to diet have a responsibility to help those who can't afford to eat.

Eating right and working out have become routine for me. I don't think about them, I just do them. But the fire in my belly that drives me to live healthy and happy today burns just as bright as it did yesterday, last year, or when I started this life-changing program years ago.

My motivation starts from within. I believe 100% in this program because it works. But like anyone else, I have days when I need a little extra motivation, so I look to my members. Their success is my success! My mission is to help others learn how to live and eat healthy, one day at a time.

# INTERNAL PUMPTITUDE

# — Chapter 4 —

# NO FEAR

*Only during hard times do people come to understand how difficult it is to be master of their feelings and thoughts.*
*—Anton Chekhov*

The natural state of the mind is to have no fear. We develop fear and create fearful behaviors and attitudes based on being told for years that we will fall short, that we will not measure up, and most likely not succeed. Parents, teachers, family members, friends, co-workers and bosses may unknowingly negatively contribute over the years. Keep in mind that while there are many human behaviors and attitudes that are built in instinctively, fear is not one of them. In this chapter, we will share many real-life stories that have taken place, where an attitude of success and achievement eclipsed the fear of risk and failure.

Everyone has some fear, so the goal is to confront that fear. Fear is simply a warning to be alert and sharp. It's not something to run from. People who have broken through their fear to thrive have performed some of the most courageous acts.

The fear of trying or of being ridiculed is a man-made fear. I was lucky enough to be constantly encouraged by my mother and grandmother to try new things, no matter what the results. But even if you didn't have that foundation, you can reclaim that power now—say no to fear and achieve your dreams!

## 17) Anything is possible

*Anything is Possible* is a weekly radio show hosted by Jack Krasula on a 50,000 watt station, WJR AM-760, *The Great Voice of the Great Lakes*.

Each one-hour show features a distinguished guest who is living an extraordinary life in the face of fear and other debilitating challenges. He or she has overcome simple beginnings and many obstacles in life to realize what seemed like unachievable dreams. In addition, each guest discusses the driving force that led them to greatness and how this journey has evolved into giving back to the community.

There is no one I've ever met with more of an appreciation for building a legacy, learning from that, and applying it to the future than Jack Krasula. Being interviewed for Jack's show in January 2013 was a highlight of my life, and the show's recording has earned a special place in my Life Chest.

When you have a chance to tell or write your life story, by the nature of reflecting on your accomplishments and all the experiences that you've had, the process itself helps to motivate and inspire you to keep going and build on what you've already achieved. As I've stated previously, life is a marathon, not a sprint (*Maximum Pumptitude*, Chapter 5, #35); no sooner have you accomplished one set of goals, than your excitement shifts to the next ones. The true learning, experience and benefit to your life is the journey, it's not the destination.

Here is a great quote from Mr. John Adams that expresses the importance of taking the time to journal, or in this case, to write your life story: "A pen is certainly an excellent instrument to fix a man's attention and to inflame his ambition."

## 18) Risk taking—nine new stores in 91 days

In July 2013, Art Van will undertake something amazing that is unlike anything in our 53-year history. In Chapter 5 of *Maximum Pumptitude*, I shared how, when I was at The Brick, we opened six large-scale furniture, appliance, mattress, and television stores in Montreal all in one day. Well, we at Art Van are going to open nine new stores in 91 days in three cities—Chicago (six Art Van Furniture stores), Toledo (one Art Van Furniture store and one PureSleep store), and Fort Wayne (one Art Van Furniture store).

Art Van Elslander, Kurt Darrow and Kim Yost

We'll cap things off in Chicago on July 18th with a ribbon cutting gala ceremony, and, to honor our Detroit roots, we will be showcasing Motown by bringing the Temptations to Chicago. This will be a store opening like no other!

Temptations with Art Van Elslander and Kim Yost

Chicago Art Van Furniture ribbon cutting ceremony, July 18, 2013

We had been developing our real estate strategy, which included opening one new store approximately every six months. It was at one of these real estate meetings that we dared to do something that, on the surface, would appear unrealistic, and that is to not only open nine new stores in 91 days, but take Art Van to three entirely new states, Illinois, Ohio and Indiana. If it wasn't for the endorsement and support of our chairman, Mr. Art Van, none of us on the Art Van leadership team would have been confident that we could pull this off. He has been charged up about this unforgettable challenge.

For months now, our real estate vice-president Steve Glucksman has been battling in the trenches to secure our leases, negotiating with some of the toughest and most ruthless landlords in America. Keep in mind, Chicago is the third-largest furniture and mattress market in North America, third only to New York and Los Angeles.

In Chapter 2, #10 of this book, we spoke about how you need to major in the majors, know the value of the prize, and focus on the dollar bills versus the pennies. Clearly, all of these new markets are dollar bills for Art Van, and the value of the prize is humongous. Now, we could write an entire book on all the operational details we've been working on and will continue to work on between now and when the first of the new stores opens in July 2013 and the last of the nine new stores opens in February 2014.

In addition to getting the locations, designing the stores, building the assortments, hiring the employees, developing the marketing plans, securing the public relations firms, and developing our supply chain and warehousing process, we also found the time, with the leadership of Amelia Ellenstein, to work on the store design of the future. We have been working with a third-part consultant, Interbrand Design Forum, on a 90,000-square-foot store that features the latest thinking for store design, store layout, visual graphics, customer service, and creating a shopping experience unequaled in our industry. This work, in whole and in part, will be introduced in these nine new stores. Imagine the financial commitment and the amount of time and effort that's going into this project! But without risk, there is no reward; such is the risk, such is the reward.

There are a lot of lessons coming from the new openings that are cascading to all our stores. There is huge energy that is generated by new ventures that touches even those people who are not directly involved. The moral of the story is that you should always be exploring new opportunities in order to refresh every other aspect of your work.

What an exciting time for us at Art Van! Several of the leadership team members are filling out daily and weekly journals, to capture this huge volume of activities and the risks we are taking. Many of the positive skills, habits and concepts from *Pumptitude*, *Maximum Pumptitude* and *Internal Pumptitude* are being channeled into these amazing projects. When we come to the podium to cut the ribbon with the governors, mayors and city council members for all these new stores, we will be bringing our entire team to a place we've never been before, and when we get there, we will never want to go back.

This was a big stretch for the Art Van leadership team, and there were doubters, right from the start. As we pressed forward, people recognized that we had passed the point of no return, and there was nowhere to go but forward. Now the doubters are seeing results just like the rest of us. They are benefitting from the rewards of stretching to a new level.

We are growing as a team and everyone is expanding his or her capacity. I love seeing them handle challenges that until recently may have been unimaginable.

## 19) Ignore the naysayers

*Everything that is good will be attacked.—Jim Rohn*

This above quote contains a valuable reminder from Jim Rohn, that for every garden, somebody will want to plant weeds; for every glass house, somebody will want to throw a rock through it. This has been going on since the beginning of time, though Jim reminds us that he was not around for the early design of this negative human behavior. So when you go upon your life and are achieving amazing things, don't be discouraged or frustrated when someone comes along and tries to tear it down. Instead, expect it! Realize the law of the naysayers and continue to forge on even when you are criticized or challenged for your success.

The important thing to remember about naysayers is that they probably put little thought into those bombs of negativity and doubt they just tossed in your path, leaving you in peril, even paralyzed. If people are thoughtless with you, don't put any thought into what they say or do.

# 20) Lifetime of achievement

*You can't create the future if you keep
focusing on the past.—Source unknown*

Once you have one success, you have to do something bigger and bolder and build on each achievement. The idea is to have stepping stones or building blocks that lead to your own personal Super Bowl, Stanley Cup, or Mount Everest. It's only once you've climbed smaller mountains that you get a true glimpse of Everest.

We all travel a virtuous circle through life, similar to the Stages of Life we explored in Chapter 11 of *Maximum Pumptitude*— we begin as a student, then we become an apprentice, then we become a rookie, then we become experienced, then we become a master, then we need to start all over again. That's how we stay fresh. There's always a new circle to complete. The best performers have an attitude called "beginner's mind"— they're always open to new learning.

Unless you constantly refresh yourself, you don't become great, you become stale. The lifetime of achievement is also a lifetime of exploration, experimentation and education. You need to always be searching for role models and being a role model. Most importantly, this personal evolution needs to be an act of joy, not a chore. Humility, not ego or status.

This ongoing development is also the best way to protect oneself against mental degradation. The brain expands in direct proportion to the challenges we set it. The greater the challenges, the more developed the brain becomes.

Crises and complex problems are gifts that expand our mental capacity. Ambition immunizes us against complacency and atrophy. We'll continue this topic in Chapter 7, #32.

## 21) Miracle morning

*You've got to get up every morning with determination if you're going to go to bed with satisfaction.—George Lorimer*

I came across an incredible story of survival and reinvention that uses a form of the "power hour" and my 23-hour day, as described in *Pumptitude*, Chapter 7. The book is *The Miracle Morning* by Hal Elrod. Years ago, Hal experienced a head-on collision in his car, resulting in paralyzing fractures throughout his body, and being pronounced clinically dead for six minutes. As he fought his way back to life, through months of rehabilitation, he came across an experience that changed his life.

Like so many of us, Hal didn't like to get up early in the morning, and he didn't like to jog. A friend of his encouraged him to do both, since he was trying to get his life back on track and get his body and mind to refocus on the future. As Hal describes in the book, he struggled to get up in the morning, and to jog, but after doing both for a few days, he immediately realized the overwhelming benefits. Over time, he created what he calls his "miracle morning."

Here is the miracle morning ritual Hal created: Every day at 5:00 a.m., for one hour, he does six activities in consecutive order. The first 10 minutes, he spends in silent meditation. In the second 10 minutes, he reads inspirational, motivational and educational books. The third 10 minutes, he spends on positive affirmations that reinforce his self-confidence and empowerment. Then he moves to 10 minutes of visualization, followed by 10 minutes of journaling, and then 10 minutes of exercise, which in his case is jogging.

Throughout the book, he describes this 60-minute ritual as nothing short of a miracle. He explains the phenomenal benefit that it's had on him and so many others. He strongly encourages his readers to embrace the miracle morning, just as I have urged you to adopt the 23-hour day by reserving one hour for exercise. Hal also shares testimonials of several people who have also adopted and are benefitting from the success of the miracle morning.

Included in his book is what Hal calls the 30-Day Life Transformation Challenge (his "fast-start kit"). Much like our 68-Day Challenge, he encourages all of us to make a decision to change, and to take action, which will result in that change.

When you get a chance to read his book, you will come to realize that Hal also believes that if you want things to change in your life, you must first be willing to make those changes. Nothing will happen without a serious commitment. I enjoyed the quote Hal shared from Anthony Robbins: "To make profound changes in your life, you need either inspiration or desperation."

If you implement the principles of Hal's miracle morning and my 23-hour day, you are guaranteed some key benefits. You are guaranteed to immediately lower your stress levels. You are guaranteed to start improving your overall health and get in the best physical shape of your life. You will also realize that living a life of purpose is far better than living one without.

So remember, by simply changing the way you wake up in the morning, you can transform every area of your life faster and with more impact than you ever thought was possible.

As you read about habits in the next chapter, especially #23, please remember the power of the miracle morning and what an amazing life changer it can be to simply replace one hour of sleep with one hour of focused revitalization.

Isn't that an amazing coincidence? I've been living the 23-hour day for over three decades of my life, and a young man came up with even a better way to utilize it, describe it, and encourage you to become it. Now let's move on to examine the power of good habits, and how they can shape and mold a great life.

## One Percenter: Oscar Miskelly, Founder, Miskelly Furniture

I met Oscar Miskelly over a decade ago in our performance group called Strivers. Right away, we hit it off and have become dear friends ever since. We often compete to see who's the funniest and who can tell the best jokes during our dinners out and at our conferences. If you were to tour his stores, you would clearly see his commitment to his team, to his customers, and ultimately to his personal growth. Put on your seatbelt; his story is sure to inspire!

||||||||||||||||||||||||||||||||||||||||||||||||||||||||||||||||||||||||||||||||||||||||||||||||||||||||||||

A 1976 graduate of Mississippi State School of Business, Oscar is active in the community through several civic and professional organizations. He currently serves as president of The Furniture Marketing Group—a 100-member buying group made up of most of the nation's top furniture retailers.

Oscar, along with brothers Chip and Tommy, founded Miskelly Furniture in 1978. Miskelly's has prospered over the past 35 years and is listed by *Furniture Today* as one of the Top 100 furniture stores in America. He credits the Lord's blessings and an incredible team for having achieved the success they have enjoyed.

||||||||||||||||||||||||||||||||||||||||||||||||||||||||||||||||||||||||||||||||||||||||||||||||||||||||||||

## The power of long-term thinking

We've all heard the phrase: You can play now and pay later or pay now and play later. How true it is! A famous Harvard study showed a direct connection between long-term thinking and success. The more people focused on short-term gains, the more likely they were to fail. Those who focus on what "feels good" right now are doomed to be unsuccessful. As a privately-owned company, we make decisions based on what's in our long-term best interest instead of reacting to any situation for a short-lived "win." That long-term view has served us well for over 35 years, particularly as it relates to our customers, employees, and vendor partners.

## Don't ever give up

When God wants to make a mushroom, he takes six hours. When He wants to make an oak tree, He takes sixty years. An oak tree is just an acorn that refuses to give up. When you set a goal, stay the course. It is always too soon to quit. You may need to alter your course of action, but don't give up. You are never a failure until you quit, and it's always too soon to quit! Just remember, **the pain of regret is greater than the pain of discipline**. While talent is important, it only provides hope for accomplishment; perseverance guarantees it. So the question is: Do you want your life to be a mushroom or an oak tree?

## Face your fear

I'm not the bravest person, but I have learned that courage is not the absence of fear, but courage is facing fear. We have faced lots of adversity in our time in business—from floods, hurricanes, and economic downturns to the everyday challenges that small businesses face. It's been through that adversity we learned to face our fear of failure head on. Calm seas don't make good sailors, so navigating these uncertain waters has made us better stewards for sure. I am no longer afraid of failure. I am only afraid of succeeding at the wrong thing.

Finally, I love what Curtis Martin, the great running back for the New England Patriots and NY Jets, said at his NFL Hall of Fame Induction speech: "It's not what you achieve in life, it's what you become in the process of those achievements."

# INTERNAL PUMPTITUDE

# — Chapter 5 —

# HABITS THAT CAN CHANGE YOUR LIFE

*Obstacles can't stop you. Problems can't stop you. Most of all, other people can't stop you. Only you can stop you.*
*—Jeffrey Gitomer*

Stephen R. Covey published two all-time bestselling books, which contain powerful lessons in personal change. In *The 7 Habits of Highly Effective People* and *The 8th Habit*, we learn about the habits and consistent behaviors that the one percenters and high achievers all have in common. I vividly remember reading my first copy of *The 7 Habits*, and immediately starting to put its principles and lessons to work.

Embracing the seven habits in many parts of my life, both personally and professionally, has had a most profound impact on my success. As a constant reminder to myself and to you, here are Covey's seven habits, which millions of people around the world have learned and are benefitting from:

1. Be proactive
2. Begin with the end in mind
3. Put first things first
4. Think win-win

5. Seek first to understand, then to be understood

6. Synergize

7. Sharpen the saw

Recently, I came across a new book, which had a similar effect on my life, and most importantly, on my personal habits. *The Power of Habit*, by Charles Duhigg, shares key learning from several research studies and real-life stories. It is clear that everything to do with our success is surrounded and contributed to by our habits. It is clear that good habits are based on self-regulatory disciplines and constant strong and never-ending willpower.

What is exciting to learn is that we can all, as life learners, develop new and positive contributing habits. But what I've learned is that the best way to develop one of these new habits is to replace an old habit. Our habits have a huge impact on everything that we do, and, as stated previously, there are compounding benefits of having daily and weekly habits (and beyond) with exercise, the foods we eat, the money we save, and the people we engage with.

By understanding what drives our behaviors, we can direct positive new behaviors, and ultimately benefit from having these new habits become automatic and sustainable without thought. Use the 68-Day Challenge or your Schmonday goal-setting process to have a good look at your own habits and your daily and weekly routines. Then look in the mirror and ask yourself, "Are these habits productive and contributing to my goals and life's mission?" If you discover that you must change some of your habits, read Duhigg's book and start today.

One of the habits Duhigg discusses in the book that I strongly recommend is delayed gratification. All too often, we lack the patience, willpower or self-control to delay any rewards or gratification related to either a project or goal we are working on. Delaying gratification is to have your intelligence overpower the control of your emotion. So the next time you want to give yourself a reward for a job well done, ensure that you only do so at the end of your accomplishment, not a moment before.

In this chapter, I will build on my own personal habits of Schmonday and daily rituals like exercise, my five daily to dos, and constantly embracing the power of the CANI.

# 22) Schmonday

In our first book, *Pumptitude*, Chapter 3, #17–21, you first came to realize the positive benefits of a habit that I developed several years ago. Good habits are everything in your success, and the habit of Schmonday enables us to concentrate and strengthen our good habits and minimize our poor habits. In fact, if there's one habit that I truly know will cause a breakthrough in everything you do, it's the weekly Schmonday habit.

My Schmonday is from 5:00–10:00 p.m. on Sundays—an eighth day of the week between Sunday and Monday that I created. Schmonday is quality time dedicated to personal development, which enables me to prepare for the start of the next week on Monday morning. You can find your own Schmonday any day of week.

I've had the fortunate opportunity to speak about the power of Schmonday to a number of executives, graduating students, business owners, colleagues and friends.

Over the last several months, I have received several personal endorsements regarding this habit. People are telling me that out of all the learning that I've shared, this one has the most impact. They say that taking the time to reflect, to read, to work on themselves has been a big boost.

Schmonday gives you the time to constantly reinvent yourself. It's like opening the window when you're driving a car and breathing fresh air into your lungs. Schmonday is about finding your own mental window in order to breathe.

Many of us live our lives in the context of constant disruption, activity, and pressing deadlines. If we don't create sustained periods of personal focus time, our lives can spin out of control.

We need to carve out our own time and focus on what's really important so we can take it on. It may be reading, writing, planning or just thinking. But it's this quiet "me time" that enables us to face the world with confidence and preparedness.

This is a habit that needs to be embedded in your seven-day rhythm. It's about taking time for yourself to reinvent yourself and your future. It's about getting off the merry-go-round to reset your compass so you don't get lost. Schmonday allows people to take back control of their life in a world that always seems to be on the verge of being out of control.

**A plan without action is a daydream, but action without a plan is a nightmare**. We need both planning and action to be the best we can be. If we act with a clear and powerful plan, we will act with the conviction, clarity and confidence that will enroll others to our cause. That creates successful results, which creates even more confidence to step up to the next level.

This generates powerful momentum that carries us past roadblocks that would stop other people in their tracks. Without momentum, everything is more difficult.

I love the quote that my mother constantly reminds me of, "Wisdom is wasted on the elderly." Her prayer for me has always been that I become as wise as I can, as early as I can, so I have the resources to do something with that wisdom. If you recall, the three great drivers for wisdom are: (1) being open for learning, (2) gaining experience and (3) reflection (*Pumptitude*, Chapter 3, #19). Reflection is something you can definitely include in your Schmonday.

Even the calls with my CEO coach Mike Lipkin are an extension of this concept. It's highly concentrated reflection time for me that is enhanced by Mike's comments. That's the power of a coach: to enrich your reflection time and magnify your learning.

My wellbeing is a direct function of creating this time for myself. I am also able to give more of myself to the people around me because of the perspective that this exercise gives me. Without time for ourselves, the time we give others is not going to be the best it can be.

It's being still so that we find the peace within. Without inner peace, we cannot calm anyone else. We also cannot maintain our control in the face of crises and challenge.

In order to lead a life of constant motion (Chapter 10, #51), we need to find a place inside ourselves that is unchanging.

## 23) Put on your shorts and go—rise and shine!

*Confirmed: He who sits the most dies the soonest.—Neil Wagner*

This was the headline of an April 2012 article in *The Atlantic*, where writer Neil Wagner goes on to say, "Another study shows that sitting is really, really, really bad for your health."

James A. Levine, M.D., Ph.D. from the Mayo Clinic expands on this by saying, "Researchers have linked sitting for long periods of time with a number of health concerns, including obesity and metabolic syndrome."

My advice? Put a piece of sandpaper in your pants and get moving! A chair is not your friend!

In Chapter 7 of *Pumptitude*, I told you all about the 23-hour day, where you have to find your one "power hour" a day to build your energy through exercise. Now, I want to remind you that all you have to do each morning or each evening is just have enough personal commitment and drive to put on your t-shirt and your shorts. Once you've done that, all your other instincts will take over. You know how important it is to exercise. You know about the benefits of exercise. You know how your health could suffer if you don't exercise. So really, how much energy is required to put on a pair of shorts and a t-shirt? Isn't it easy? Right! It really is all about dealing with your health, one hour and one day at a time.

Here's another note about putting on your shorts and t-shirt. I recently bought a new pair of bright florescent red Nike Air Max shoes and a matching bright florescent red Nike t-shirt. When people see me out running in these, they call out to me about how they like the shoes and shirt, and how it looks like I'm on fire. Interestingly enough, when I started running in these bright florescent red shirt and shoes, seeing my glowing red feet underneath me, I noticed I was running faster. So when you're selecting your exercise gear, go bold, go colorful, and light yourself on fire!

In *Pumptitude* (Chapter 7), we talked about how creating a 23-hour day by reserving a power hour for exercise delivers a powerful ROI (return on investment) and ROE (return on energy). I also want to remind you that if you create this disciplined habit, you will also benefit from the ROA (return on attitude), ROR (return on results), ROS (return on success), and lastly, the greatest ROI of all—ROL (return on life)!

Back in Chapter 1, I shared the power of the 68-Day Challenge and how developing new habits can have a profound impact on your life. You give me one hour, every day, of any type of activity, and I guarantee it will change your life. Recently, while I was running with Donna one morning, she fired up her iPhone and started to play a series of motivational videos from YouTube. By this time, I was about 30 minutes into my workout and already excited to get pumped up for the remainder. Here is some of the learning I got from listening to these videos while we ran:

- Pick up your feet and move as if they're on fire.

- Fire up your heart, your head, and your butt, and get on with it.

- Welcome to the grind (in #24, I'll share that you need to have a *passion for the grind*).

- Don't listen to your body, don't ask your body for its opinion because it will be the devil on your shoulder that says, "I have pains, I have aches, and why the hell are you doing this to me?" If you listen to your body, it will mislead you.

- You need to turn your back to what makes common sense, face the enemy within, and continue the drive.

When you wake up in the morning, you need to sit up, put your feet on the ground, and get ready to work your butt off! The easy way is not for you. You are driven by your goals, your ambition, and your drive for success. Pain is temporary, and if you give into it, the likelihood is that you won't achieve your dreams.

Go beyond that little pain, that little discomfort, and continue to tell yourself that you can become and achieve anything that you put the energy behind. Continue to tell yourself that you are not going to finish where you began. Tell yourself that you can become what you absolutely know you can become.

Failure can destroy you or it can make you stronger. It will make you work harder; it will mold you and shape you. Failure will lead you to win. Start your life's race every morning. You're playing for the ultimate victory—your victory over yourself.

**No excuses**. I want to put the fear of the devil in you. I want you to be scared of what you will not become if you don't put in the effort. Success is getting up one more time, one more day, and putting in the effort. Prove it to yourself; you have it within you to develop this strong habit. Every winner has had failures— many of them—but what they don't do is make excuses. They get up every morning and every day with a never-ending drive and pursuit of success.

You must drive procrastination out of thoughts and stop saying you'll do it tomorrow. Becoming the best you can be has no finish line and nothing else matters. So rise and shine and become the star that you know you can be.

## 24) Discipline—passion for the grind

*You can't make footprints in the sands of time if you're sitting on your butt. And who wants to make butt prints in the sands of time?*—Bob Moawad

Getting up every morning and grinding it out isn't always fun. Sometimes it's tedious or downright hard work. I'm sure you can relate to that from your own life. Yet, every one percenter and top performer has a *passion* for the grind. Olympic athletes have to train hours and hours every day, week after week, month after month to meet their goal. Salespeople have to be on their game every time they come in contact with a customer, and boy can that be a grind. The great ones approach the grind with passion, rather than frustration or anguish.

Having a passion for the grind will help you sharpen yourself through the grind. Without a passion for the grind, the grind will wear you away. We have to get up every morning and know that we will face challenges. We need to prepare ourselves mentally, emotionally and physically to face the day.

Author James Michener said:

> *The master in the art of living makes little distinction between his work and his play, his labor and his leisure, his mind and his body, his information and his recreation, his love, and his religion. He hardly knows which is which. He simply pursues his vision of excellence at whatever he does, leaving others to decide whether he is working or playing. To him he's always doing both.*

## 25) Compounding benefits—a win is a win

*Become living proof of what investing in yourself can create.—Mike Lipkin*

There is no difference between a small win and a big win. A win is a win. Every win is a deposit in the self-belief account. By winning in one space, your confidence is expanded in another space. It's like ever-widening ripples of power and personal impact. Whether you throw a boulder or a pebble into a pond, it still causes ripples. Begin with a pebble. Every act is a cause set in motion. When you seize an opportunity, you never know how far it will go. What you deposit in effort today will have compounding benefits in your successes tomorrow.

## 26) Goal setting—set yourself in motion

*By recording your dreams and goals on paper, you set in motion the process of becoming the person you most want to be. Put your future in good hands— your own.—Mark Victor Hansen*

We covered the important topic of goal setting in Chapter 6 of *Pumptitude*. In making a great life, goals are clear contributors to our evolution of change and improvement. Goals, properly articulated, and fully visualized, help us design the future in a much clearer state. By writing our goals down, it helps clear the path and allows us to stay focused on our dreams. Goals are like magnets; they pull us forward.

Your goals affect everything in your life. They affect your attitude, they affect your work, they affect your style, they affect your success or failure, they affect your activities, and, surprisingly, your goals affect everyone around you.

Don't just settle for an existence, use goal setting to design an amazing future and life.

Here are my top six habits for achieving my goals, along with some learning I've incorporated from the works of Jim Rohn and Gary Ryan Blair.

1. **Focus**: Decide what you want and write it down. Make a list. Only include the goals that will truly change your life. The list needs to be a clear, brightly burning picture of the future. Set goals that will make you stretch, live in the danger zone, and push you to places you've never been before. Don't join the easy club. If you don't set challenging goals, the likelihood is you won't accomplish much.

2. **The five to-dos**: Review *Pumptitude*, Chapter 6, #39, "Top Five Daily Doers." There's great power in setting five clear objectives for yourself each day and relentlessly pursuing those goals until they are complete. Use this method to challenge yourself daily and weekly to get things done. These lists can be effective reminders for short-term goals.

3. **Sharing**: We all require a strong desire to share. By sharing our goals and our dreams, we inspire other people to do the same. One warning: When people can't do something themselves, they will often tell you that you can't do it either. So as much as we want to share our goals with the people around us, when we get feedback that limits us, we must learn to ignore it and push on.

4. **Relentless pursuit**: Success requires both talent and skill, and the only way to build skill is with hard work, focus and a passion for the grind. There is no easy way around it. **My relentless pursuit is my I-Pump**. When people are sleeping, I'm up running at 5:30 a.m. When others are on the golf course on Sunday afternoon,

I'm working my Schmonday. When others are thinking and pondering, I've already decided. When people are waiting and wanting, I'm already on will. I will outwork others, and I put more effort into the things that I want to get done.

5. **Winning is better than losing**: How much more seriously would you approach your goals if your life depended on them? Your income, skills and habits will be a direct reflection of your goals and commitment to personal development. You have an untapped talent; you have potential within that you will only come to realize by setting goals, striving to achieve them, and then moving forward. When you want something badly enough and you're prepared to put the effort in, the likelihood is you will achieve it. So love the feeling of being a winner. The joy of being in constant pursuit of your goals will draw you to the Winners' Circle countless times.

6. **Ego and self-esteem**: Jim Rohn asks, "What kind of person do I have to become to get all I want?" How will achieving your goal change you? The great value of life is not what you achieve, it is what you become. This is what makes you truly valuable. What skills, habits, studying, learning and other efforts are needed for the relentless pursuit of becoming the person you want to become? Imagine how those activities will enhance your self-worth!

Now that we've had a closer look at goal setting, what are you waiting for? Are you waiting for something to do? Well, if so, do it now! Become all you can become today. Goal setting is all about changing. What we've talked about throughout this book is that change can happen instantly. So do it today. Become all you can become. Success is not in short supply; it's for everyone. We are all meant to shine. Have a kid's mind and believe that you can do anything. You will be unstoppable.

*Success isn't given. It's earned.*
*On the [sales floor, in the showroom],*
*on the track, on the field, in the gym.*
*With blood, sweat, and the occasional*
*tear.—Nike (I added "the sales floor"*
*and "the showroom.")*

In this next chapter, you will read about some of my most exciting experiences and my true passion for creativity—if you use it, you can grow it. So get ready for a chapter like no other, and one of my favorite stories: Black Friday comes to Canada.

## One Percenter: Troy Davis, President, The Dufresne Group (TDG)

Years ago, I interviewed Troy Davis as a potential executive for The Brick organization. In hiring hundreds of executives, I've never hired somebody as quickly. Ten minutes into the interview, the CFO and I gave him the job. Troy and I faced many great challenges, including opening six stores in Montreal in a single day (read the story in *Maximum Pumptitude*, Chapter 5, #38). We have become great friends, and now I cheerlead his career. Both personally and professionally, he constantly takes his game to the next level. You are sure to enjoy reading about some of the habits that he has integrated into his success equation, such as the 23-hour day and Schmonday.

||||||||||||||||||||||||||||||||||||||||||||||||||||||||||||||||||||||||||||||||||||||||||||||||||||||

Troy Davis has made a career out of finding opportunities and attacking new challenges. Troy is responsible for the retail operations of TDG's two brands, 23 storefronts, a retail buying group with 100 plus storefronts, and a wholesale contract with the North West Company. During his time as president, TDG has successfully expanded its portfolio to include an additional three brands and 19 storefronts across the mid-south and launched the Dream Experience, a new mattress concept. Prior to joining TDG, Troy was the chief operating officer for The Brick, despite not having a background in retail furniture. Today, when not busy at the office or hanging out with his family, Troy can be found challenging his fitness level and living the 23-hour day.

||||||||||||||||||||||||||||||||||||||||||||||||||||||||||||||||||||||||||||||||||||||||||||||||||||||

I lead a team and support colleagues who are capable of great accomplishments and who need the drive and push to do the things they are not doing in order to achieve the results that they want. This motivates me to operate at my very best each and every day, which I do by investing in myself with mental nutrition and by pumping up my energy with a commitment to the 23-hour day.

I have always prided myself on trying to give more and add greater value then what was expected, rather than focusing on the rewards. In *Pumptitude*, this is referred to as "creating wealth" and this has served me well in growing my career and creating a great life.

In my quest to make a great life, I have actively tried to remain "open for business," to "check my ego at the door," to take feedback constructively, and to learn from the great people and mentors I have been privileged to have in my life. Two concepts that have truly made a difference for me were covered in *Pumptitude*. Both

"Schmonday" and the "Power of AND" have helped me balance and define my professional brand as an executive and my personal brand as a husband, father and friend. Schmonday, or creating an eighth day of the week, continues to be a difference maker in my career and in my personal life, as I set aside time to identify, focus, reflect, and invest in my priorities.

The Power of AND has proven instrumental in my ability to accomplish more without having to choose between this OR that. As a family man with a wonderful wife Faye and two young sons, Ryan and Cole, the Power of AND has allowed me to be a bigger part of their lives. While other parents sometimes tease while I scan reports or use my laptop in the stands during the boy's off-ice shifts, the Power of AND allows me to have fun and be present in my family's lives when it counts AND accomplish my professional obligations and goals.

No matter our situation, we all have the ability to achieve our goals and create a great life.

— Chapter 6 —

# CREATIVITY IS A CURSE

*The enemy of learning is knowing.*
*—Gary Van*

Creativity is a curse because it makes one enthusiastic to make things bigger and better. A curious person gets no rest. Yet, creativity is a curse one should be grateful to have. Ignorance may be bliss, but we don't want it. Creativity may be a curse, but we do want it!

## 27) Curiosity

Several years ago, I had the opportunity to meet the founder and owner of Future Shop Canada, whom we nicknamed Mr. K. He told me there was nothing free in life except for one thing— asking questions. He indicated that a high-quality question, with a great answer, has the potential to unlock an amazing future. Therefore, being curious and having an ambition to discover the wonders of the world rather than being the person who knows it all is the true learning here. Having an inquiring and curious mind is a trait of a one percenter and high achiever.

One percenters have an enquiring mind. They need to know. They want to get under the surface. It's not good enough for them just to be told something; they need to explore the truth for themselves. The more they understand, the more they can add their own creativity. They take existing ideas and make them better. They never take things for granted. They investigate. They are detectives of opportunity.

Some of the most powerful questions are the simplest ones, such as, "What do you think?" (People love to be asked for their opinions!) Dale Carnegie said that people who are interested in other people are interesting to other people. Achievers are in constant question mode. They are in a state of exploration and fascination. They are liberated by the wonder of discovery rather than the burden of knowing it all. People who know it all feel like they have to do all the talking. Therefore, they never learn and they never grow. Curiosity is the most direct route to becoming and staying a one percenter.

Bobby Kennedy said, "There are those that look at things the way they are, and ask why? I dream of things that never were, and ask why not?"

When I was a young buyer in my mid-20s, I developed a skill and then ultimately a reputation for being a "stone turner." Mr. Bill Campbell, a dear friend of mine and sales representative for many different furniture brands, taught me how to turn every stone I possibly could, seeking new and different items, new and different concepts, and ultimately new ideas. I would go into showrooms and look in more corners, look at more product, and ask more questions than any of my contemporaries. I was always curious in a way that many weren't.

By constantly turning stones, I was able to come up with several items and concepts that wouldn't have come to light had I not been such a digger. I believe the skill of being a stone turner gave me a clear, unfair advantage over the other buyers I competed with. So in addition to having a curious mind and always asking questions, master the skill of being a stone turner. You just never know what you will uncover.

# 28) Parking lot to luxury furniture store—see what can be

As I wrote in our previous book, *Maximum Pumptitude*, a key to success is being able to see something that others can't. This can be a huge advantage in not only driving your creativity, but your results. In Chapter 10, #59, I talked about hockey legend Wayne Gretzky, who could see where the puck was going next and be there before anyone else on the ice, and Steve Jobs, who saw how people would be using computers in the future and then took us there. I also shared my own story of seeing a vision, jotting it down on a napkin, then following through with relentless tenacity until it came to life as Home Show Canada (Chapter 5, #38).

Here is another great story that follows the same concept. Mr. Art Van and I had been trying to put together a flagship location for a luxury furniture store called Scott Shuptrine. Gary Van, our president, had operated a chain of these luxury furniture stores in Michigan several years back and closed them approximately five years ago. Over the past several years, we've had countless requests to bring back the Scott Shuptrine brand to southeast Michigan. Now, the best location for this Scott's store was in the Birmingham/Royal Oak area of southeast Michigan. After several months of looking for a suitable location, we found that they were either too big or too small, or the rent structures didn't make any sense. We were truly committed to finding a location in Birmingham, particularly on Woodward Avenue, the main road that runs for miles through Birmingham and Royal Oak.

On one Sunday morning, after driving for miles up and down Woodward Avenue, it was clear that we had to think outside the box for this solution. It was on this Sunday morning, stopping across the street from our existing Art Van store, that the innovative solution came to us. The existing Art Van store, built years ago, had two levels, with the furniture and mattress store on the second level, and over 200 parking stalls on the ground level. Looking across at this store, we saw something that didn't exist, and that was to take the north side of that ground-level parking lot and turn it into a 13,000-square-foot luxury Scott's furniture store.

Just as Michelangelo looked at the slab of marble and saw the statue of David within, we saw an amazing luxury furniture store where nobody else would have ever seen it.

Later in this book (Chapter 10, #54), I'm going to share the importance of every individual and business being an adoption agency. This was a classic example of the Art Van team adopting a truly new idea. Once given the idea, Vice President of Brand Strategy and Store Environment Amelia Ellenstein set upon an amazing path to not only design but build this store. Over a series of activities, starting from permit approvals right to the ground-breaking ceremony and the ribbon-cutting, her team's creativity and sheer genius applied. Other Art Van executives needed to adopt this child as well, including our buyer Terry Browning, who spent a year putting together 60 of the most incredible room settings you could believe.

Amelia remembers that not only was the location a parking lot, but the structure required tremendous creativity to overcome— four-foot concrete columns and six-foot concrete headers all supported the second floor and had to be integrated into the design. Not to mention the fact that the ground was not graded, but sloped upward!

On the following pages, you'll see several photographs of Scott's on Woodward Avenue. As you look through them, remember that this all started with a vision that took us from a parking lot to a luxury furniture store in just a few months. This was a story about taking risks to bring that vision to fruition. These were the efforts of several people working together with a common focus and goal, staying focused on a tight schedule to accomplish something in a very short amount of time. The outcome was truly extraordinary.

The grand, custom stairway that connects the Scott's gallery to the upstairs Art Van Furniture store is a dramatic centerpiece in the space.

The ceiling beam structure, inspired by the veins found in a leaf, works to create intimacy in the store, while maintaining an open ceiling that creates visual volume despite the small square footage.

The custom concrete floor is speckled with gold, bronze, and metal shake to harken the humble sophistication of Mother Nature's natural metals.

Architect
Mike Rupert

Interior Designer
Courtney Finn

Architect
Svetlana Vrubel

General Contractor
Joe Maiorano

Supervisor Graphic Design
Kimmie Parker

Key contributors to the design and development of Scott Shuptrine Interiors

# 29) Black Friday comes to Canada

What you're about to read is a story of epic proportion, a story that fits well into this chapter, "Creativity is a Curse." It also incorporates much of the learning that we're sharing in our *Pumptitude* series of books, such as be relentless, think differently, develop an adoption agency, competition is the elevator to success, we must change the world as we see it, and one percenters can make a difference.

It was November 23, 2007, America's single-largest shopping day known as Black Friday. At that time, I was CEO and president of The Brick, Canada's largest furniture, appliance, mattress and electronics retailer. I was at our head office in Edmonton, Alberta, Canada when I received a call from the chairman of the board, Mr. Ron Barbaro. Mr. Barbaro had an apartment in downtown Manhattan and went there each Black Friday to join 360 million other shoppers for outstanding deals and crazy savings.

Now, Black Friday has a unique history. Decades ago, an American president moved Thanksgiving to Thursday, making Friday a shopping holiday. The reason it's called Black Friday is because this was an opportunity for American retailers to start their "golden quarter" and move from losing money—there was a depression at the time—to making money and getting out of the red and back into the black. For decades now, Canadians have been crossing the border to shop this American iconic sale. Easy to imagine when you consider that 80 percent of Canadians live within a few hours drive from the American border.

As I spoke to Mr. Barbaro several times that day, hearing about the line-ups, crazy deals, and sheer excitement happening throughout America's retail stores, an idea started to form. What if Canadians no longer had to go across the border in that third week of November to shop the American Black Friday? We would bring Black Friday to Canada! On the surface, this may sound like a daunting and unrealistic goal given that Black Friday was the American sale of the year. After all, Canada had its Boxing Day, the day after Christmas. Although it was never written about or spoken amongst the great retailers on both sides of the border, in my 30 years as a Canadian retailer, it was clear that they had their Black Friday, and we had our Boxing Day. Well, ladies and gentlemen, this was about to change.

I yelled out from my office to my associate Bridgette Dunphy to get ready because we were about to create a Canadian Black Friday that would take place a year from now in November 28, 2008, and that from now until then, she and I were going to call, write, inspire, motivate and threaten every Canadian retailer across the country to participate in the first ever Canadian Black Friday. Through the months, we placed calls, we sent emails, and we developed a plan. To ensure the success of our first ever Black Friday, we got several major retailers to join in, including, of course, The Brick.

One point of interest is that throughout the fall of 2008, several major Canadian retailers, including Sears Canada, were bitterly complaining about the amount of Canadian cross-border shopping and were petitioning the Canadian government to increase duty fees in order to significantly reduce the amount of Canadians going to the U.S. to shop.

In the fall of 2009, I relocated to Michigan and started working with the Art Van team. But from that first sale in the fall of 2008 until last year, year after year, more Canadian retailers have joined in and I'm pleased to say that I received several emails and phone calls like this one from Troy Davis, whom you met at the end of Chapter 5:

> Kim, I am pleased to report that Black Friday has soared to new heights in Canada and continues to build year after year. Major retailers from all sectors continue to jump on board. We posted a 191 percent lift in sales yesterday over our previous Black Friday total (and last year was a record). I want to reach out to say thanks for inspiring and helping to pave the way to creating a great retail day.

Even Wal-Mart Canada was on board!

I heard an incredible amount of objections from people who couldn't believe that the Canadians could ever compete on Black Friday; there were top executives who couldn't adopt the vision and politicians who wouldn't make the date a shopping holiday. Let me share an account of one response that really surprised me.

Down the road from the corporate office at The Brick in Edmonton, Alberta is the West Edmonton Mall—millions of retail square feet under one roof, 20 million shoppers annually. In the spring of 2008, I called their ownership and told them that for years, shoppers were parking their cars in West Edmonton Mall's parking lot, only to board tour buses with promotional companies who would take these busloads of shoppers from Edmonton four hours south to shop Black Friday in the U.S. Surely, West Edmonton Mall would embrace the new Canadian Black Friday. Yet the response was no. They just couldn't imagine that we could compete with the historic American Black Friday.

This was definitely not the case; over the past years, Canadian retailers have joined one at a time, to the extent that in fall 2012, Canadian retailers put on a full-out assault on America's Black Friday, bringing the all-new sale nationally to Canada.

Meanwhile, in November 2009, I participated in my first ever American Black Friday at Art Van, when we broke an all-time record for Black Friday. Kevin Gilfillan wrote about this in a letter featured in Chapter 13 of *Maximum Pumptitude*. I'm pleased to say that with the drive and competitiveness of the entire Art Van team, we have since broken that record in 2010, 2011 and 2012. God bless Black Friday!

I'm now leading a charge for us here in the U.S. to compete with Canada for Boxing Day. In the U.S., we call this the "Day after Christmas Sale," but I won't rest until we officially call it Boxing Day, America's second-biggest retail day to Black Friday. Remember, competition is the elevator to success (*Maximum Pumptitude*, Chapter 6, #42).

Imagine that one obscure Canadian retailer could take on the American Black Friday and change Canadians' shopping habits. Imagine the compounding sales Canadian retailers will achieve in future years, all because I had an idea and relentlessly pursued that idea until it was realized.

In hearing this story, my CEO coach Mike Lipkin summed up the key principles that were at work in this success.

- I had an idea.

- I took immediate action on the idea.

- I talked to as many people as possible about the idea.

- I packaged the idea to a group of key players.

- I built a network that acted as one.

- I established the idea as a ritual that grew stronger every year.

## 30) This is the time to act—only action is rewarded

*An ounce of performance is worth pounds of promises.—Kevin Gilfillan*

In his article *The Time to React*, Jim Rohn writes, "Engaging in genuine discipline requires that you develop the ability to take action. You don't need to be hasty if it isn't required, but you don't want to lose much time either." He says that by delaying action, you'll lose momentum as your desire fades, until your passion grows cold.

When you hear something or read something that inspires you, Rohn says, "You've got to take action; otherwise the wisdom is wasted. The emotion soon passes unless you apply it to a disciplined activity." Discipline, he says, is key to starting a new life process and habit. Rohn also calls this the "Law of Diminishing Intent."

## 31) See into the future—become a first spotter

In *Maximum Pumptitude*, Chapter 10, #59, Anticipate the future, we talk about how history has shown us that when a one percenter can see into the future, and it becomes reality, they are miles ahead. I want to build on this concept in being a *first spotter*—traveling above the fray and seeing well beyond the vision of others. Many books have been published on trends, human behavior, and the psychology of current generations. All of these can be very helpful in anticipating the trends, the demands, and the opportunities going forward. Taking time on a regular basis to think beyond will give you one of your greatest returns on energy and time.

Living in Detroit, I'm constantly reminded about how a visionary, Mr. Henry Ford, approached the future. When he asked his customers what they wanted, they all wanted a faster horse that ate less. What he gave them, was not a horse, but a Model T automobile.

The hardest things to see are things that are not there yet. The power is in the ability to anticipate what is about to happen. It's about searching for the future, not looking back at the past. In olden times, the tall ships always had a lookout on top of the mast. Today, we all need to be spotters and see what others cannot yet see.

If other people are going to listen to you, you must communicate your predictions effectively. Beware of the curse of Cassandra! In Greek mythology, Cassandra was the daughter of King Priam and Queen Hecuba of Troy. Her beauty caused Apollo to grant her the gift of prophecy. When Cassandra refused Apollo's attempted seduction, he placed a curse on her so that her predictions and those of all her descendants would not be believed. She is a figure both of the epic tradition and of tragedy.

As much as it is vitally important to see into the future, let's all remember that learning from the past is as equally important. If we spend more time analyzing mistakes we made and come to understand what we could have done differently, this helps us move forward positively toward future successes. Here's a funny saying that Bill Comrie used when we looked back on our fond memories: "We never remember the outhouse at the cabin when we reflect on the good old days." Keep in mind, the good old days are the same days we are in today. The same challenges that we forget we faced in the past, are the ones we are facing today.

Well, we're getting close to the halfway mark in our third and final book in the *Pumptitude* series. Keep reading; there's much more to come. You'll really enjoy our chapter about change, and its necessity in all our lives.

## Art Van One Percenter: Cathy DiSante, Vice President, Advertising

When it comes to passion and creativity, one percenter Cathy DiSante has no equal. For close to three decades at Art Van, she has contributed in ways like no other. In her story, you will see she gets that it's about changing the news, rather than just reading or understanding the news (*Pumptitude*, Chapter 6, 34). She has been one of the biggest supporters of some of my craziest ideas. In addition to her own success story, she is a great one for adopting other people's children, i.e., their ideas.

GARY —
So happy to work for you
AND the entire VAN
FAMILY —

Cathy

II

After 12 great years in advertising at Hudson's department store, a merger moved all corporate offices, with me included, to Minneapolis. But after six months, I returned to Michigan and set out to work for the next-biggest retail chain. I found my spot at Art Van as head of advertising.

In my 28 years with Art Van, I've been involved with most of the changes and dynamic growth of the company. Fifteen stores have grown into 45 plus; the birth of the Clearance Center—a store within a store; free-standing PureSleep locations, franchise stores, affiliate partners, 100-page catalogs, website and e-commerce, award-winning advertising campaigns, plenty of record-breaking promotional events, and an expansion in the Midwest. New stores, new merchandise strategies, new markets, and new ways to reach the marketplace.

IIIIIIIIIIIIIIIIIIIIIIIIIIIIIIIIIIIIIIIIIIIIIIIIIIIIIIIIIIIIIIIIIIIIIIIIIIIIIIIIIIIIIIIIIIIIIIIIIIIIIIIIIIIIIIIIIIIIIIII

## Play to win!

Years ago, we had a speaker at a management conference. He was supposed to be motivational, inspirational and equipped with all the answers. A former CEO of a major company, he was retired and had been away from the action for so long that he gave a canned presentation full of family slides, including his dog, and cute little stories that solicited an occasional laugh.

Our company was going through a rough patch. Our "Changing the Game" initiative was breathing its last breath. Business was tough! Our ship was going in circles instead of on a charted path. I wanted to pull something out of our speaker if indeed he had any answers. I asked, "What do you do when business is tough and morale is low—how do you get people excited and engaged?" His answer was, "What would *you* do?" A cop-out on his part, but I replied without thinking, "Celebrate the small victories." As it turned out, I didn't pull the answer out of him; I pulled it out of me.

Let's face it; it's more fun when you're winning than when you're not. Victories (even little ones) get people energized! They can pull the team together to build bigger wins. You can play to play or you can play to win. Who doesn't like to break records, better their best, do it bigger, do it differently, and then celebrate the achievements of a team effort? When it happens, you crave more. The "retail game" is fast-paced, immediate, and ever-changing. You don't have to wait long to see if what you're contributing to the game is contributing to a win. Like a sport, it's all about the stats. The numbers tell the story! When the numbers are good, records are being broken, and you've created something new and unique, you celebrate! That, combined with the explosive energy of a team victory, carries you through to the next game.

# — Chapter 7 —

# EMBRACE CHANGE

*A person who never made a mistake
never tried anything new.*
*—Albert Einstein*

The subject of change has been covered by hundreds of authors because embracing change is such an important part of making a great life, both personally and professionally. If there's no pain, there's no change. In this chapter, you'll read several stories, new concepts, and new encouragement to embrace the change that is needed in all of our lives.

## 32) Change your thinking, change your words, change your life

The brain is a plastic, living organ that can actually change its own structure and function, even into old age. The brain is not, as was previously thought, "hardwired" like a computer. The science of neuroplasticity has expanded our understanding of the healthy brain and the resilience of human nature. Norman Doidge MD, a psychiatrist and researcher, set out to investigate neuroplasticity and met both the brilliant scientists championing it and the people whose lives they've transformed. We now know that our thoughts can actually switch our genes on and off, altering our brain anatomy.

Doidge takes us into terrain that might seem fantastic, where scientists have developed machines that can follow these physical changes in order to read people's thoughts, allowing the paralyzed to control computers and electronics just by thinking. We learn how people of average intelligence can, with brain exercises, improve their cognition and perception in order to become savant calculators, develop muscle strength, or learn to play a musical instrument, simply by imagining doing so.

When someone asks me how I am, I always reply with one or more of these words: amazing, extraordinary, remarkable. By expressing my mood in this way, it helps me feel this way. We become the language that we use. We live in the state that we create.

Too many people are victims in their own world and therefore they cannot influence others. We can create our own world and be the champion of that world. Our words define our worlds. Great achievers use great language. Words begin in the mind and are then translated into reality. If you use words like *inspire*, *grow* and *more* (our favorites from Chapter 1, #2), you materialize those realities.

Don't dig a hole with your mouth; build a springboard with your language. Great accomplishments begin with thinking and then progress to talking and doing.

Choose your thoughts carefully. We have a first mind that chooses the thought, and we have a second mind that decides what to do about it. We have to have new thinking. It's like a starter motor that ignites the rest of the machine into gear. We all have the power to change our thinking if we're open to it. When we do that, we can get to fifth gear from first and accelerate our progress to amazing places.

It doesn't take years to change. It can take years to make the decision to change. Once we decide to change, we can take the right actions. The challenge comes when there is something we know we must change, but we're not changing.

Decisions are decisive. Once they're made, the future can be seized. You cannot make a decision from an indecisive state. You need to be all in. Decisiveness is one of my hallmarks. I may be wrong sometimes, but I never doubt my decisions. We need to be deliberate. If you try to sit on the fence, it can be painful.

## 33) Living with style

For years, I have known the importance of living with style in continuing to build your personal brand. The following three stories will illustrate the value that living with style can have in your life. So let's get started.

Jim Rohn tells a story of a father who for years put his two daughters through a huge ordeal every time they wanted to go to a concert. This father would complain bitterly about how the girls dressed, how they did their hair, and all the concerns he had about them going to a rock concert, including their safety. Now, he knew as well as the girls did that once he was done putting his daughters through this grueling process of asking for money to go to the concerts, he would always eventually give in and pay for the tickets. It was after attending one of Jim Rohn's presentations and learning about living with style that this father elected to make a change. Here's what he did the next time he heard about an exciting concert he knew his daughters would want to see.

Knowing full well that he was going to buy the tickets anyway, he bought a pair of front-row tickets before they even asked. He wrote a special card to each of them, encouraging them to enjoy the seats and the concert and enclosed a ticket in each of the cards. Of course, they were thrilled—and surprised!

When his daughters arrived home from the concert, they rushed through the door, embraced their father, and told him he was the best dad on the planet. They had a wonderful time at the concert, and said it was one of the best nights of their lives.

Imagine the paradigm of his new approach. In many ways, nothing had changed. He purchased the tickets, like he had done before. His daughters went to the concert, like they had many times before. But with his new approach, this father realized the overwhelming benefit of living with style. Prior to hearing Jim Rohn's speech, he would begrudgingly give the tickets. When he treated the concert—and his daughters—as something special and made a ceremony out of how he gave the tickets, this provided a much more positive experience.

Our second story on living with style is more practical in terms of dressing for success and contributing in a positive way to your personal brand. The best example I can give you here is my wife Donna and her passion for shoes. Donna has taken her love of shoes to such a level that everyone who knows her now looks forward to seeing the various shoes that Donna may be wearing for banquets, business meetings, and on many kinds of trips. Donna came to realize that her selection of shoes was a signature that left a lasting impression on many people; so, over the past several years, she's continued to build on this, and there is no question she has taken an article of clothing that many consider just a necessity, to a much higher level that establishes her as a style setter and someone who lives to delight.

Mr. Art Van, who you have come to know, is another individual who has an unparalleled passion for style. He dressed for success well before he became successful. Every aspect of his life, not only dress, but also the decorating of his homes, exudes style. His attention to detail about his appearance has positively influenced our entire organization for over five decades. Our leadership and sales teams dress and carry themselves as if they were right out of a fashion magazine.

Jim Rohn reminds us that your appearance is everything. Although we are told never to judge a book by its cover nor superficially judge someone by their appearance, it takes hours to read a book, it takes months to get to know someone, and the reality is that you only get seconds to make a decision about both the cover and someone's appearance.

Art Van Chairman's Circle and Presidents Club Members

Everything about your style, and particularly your appearance, speaks volumes about who you are. Eventually, of course, people will get to know your insides. In the meantime, one human trait that none of us will change is that we are judged, within seconds, about how we look, how we carry ourselves, how we speak, and how we introduce ourselves. It's a whole style package.

Another form of living with style is appreciation—saying thank you. We will all go through life receiving gifts, special experiences, and many other rewarding activities given to us by others. It only takes a few minutes to thank the people who are so kind to us, and to do so with a little bit of style. Selecting the thank you card, handwriting it, picking a small gift that's unique to the person, delivering it personally, and adding some humor can express your appreciation for someone doing something nice for you while illustrating your level of style.

Your conscious decisions, each and every day, and the way you go about everything about your life, speaks volumes to your level of style. So whether it's the way you give gifts, or the way you thank people for the great things you will receive, the way you dress, or the way you greet people, let's make it lasting, let's make an outstanding impression, and let's do it with color and style. Living with style will also have a positive impact on the people around you. You will influence others to raise their level of style; although, while you see this happening, you may not realize it came from you.

## 34) Losing it and getting it back

How many people tend to go through life building a really exciting career or personal life, only to lose it and then question whether they're doing the right thing? It can happen at any age, even to a young student choosing a focus of study or a career path. We saw it in that movie, *The Seven-Year Itch*, where Marilyn Monroe stands over the subway grate and her dress flies up. Tom Ewell's character was going through a mid-life crisis of sorts, but that moment re-kindled the spark in his life. For whatever reason, seeing Marilyn Monroe was that one crucial moment that empowered a new beginning.

There are many stories of people who falter, lose traction, and wane in their focus. What is remarkable is that for each and every one of us there is that one moment, when we are ready, that can put us back on track. It is so important to pay attention to that moment and do something about it when the enthusiasm is there. Action is required, or that moment may fade and if it does, will you be there to recognize it if it appears again?

My advice is that you don't waste opportunities. Strike while they are hot! I say this often to myself and many others, *today can be the first day of the rest of your life*.

## 35) Changeology—the science of personal change

While I was writing this book, I-Pump, I received an executive book summary from Soundview for *Changeology* by John C. Norcross, PhD, a leading authority on the science of personal change. I couldn't wait to read this book, given that the whole *Pumptitude* series is all about change. His five steps to realizing your goals and resolutions will pump up your 68-Day Challenge and your year-over-year reinvention.

Here is my take on these techniques:

1. **Getting ready**: Once you have selected whatever behavior or behaviors you want to change, make sure it is about *you*, not about what others say they want changed about you. Set up a reporting system that allows you to measure your progress, otherwise there will be no urgency in your achievement. Be realistic, we hear this over and over, because so many people overstate and underachieve. Do not set yourself up for a failure. Make sure you are controlling the outcome, and that's why this change must be about you. You can't change the world but you can change what you affect in the world. Choose something positive and know how it will positively change the world. Get excited about that, so your emotions transfer to your team and they become equally motivated to change. Arm yourself with the knowledge and tools you need to make these changes. Keep your goal near and repeat, repeat, repeat. The more you believe you can, you can. Move past fear, move past your comfort zone, but stay close to your change team!

2. **Planning before leaping**: This gets you prepared to succeed. Find out what you may need to achieve your goal and get it all in place. If your goal is to lose weight, clean out your cupboards and fridge before you start. Buy the veggies and fruit and write out your meal plans for the week. Then make your goal public. Announce what you are planning, when you are starting, when you will achieve what, in how many steps (realizing smaller goals will help you actualize greater goals), and who will be helping you. Track your progress.

3. **Taking action**: Make sure you do what you say you are going to do. If you falter, talk about it with your change team, and start again where you left off. Do not quit. Quitting is not for you. Build on your preferred behaviors. Reward yourself with each achievement and report these stepping stones to your change team. Keep moving forward!

4. **Managing slips**: Get rid of unhealthy thinking patterns. Reward the advancements, analyze the slip-ups. Control the environment so you are surrounded by possibility instead of temptation. If you slip, start the next minute anew. Change your thinking, and support yourself with positive talk around what you are focused on achieving. Protect your goal—don't let triggers tilt the behavior into a consequence.

5. **Maintaining change**: Keep using your strategy even after your goal is achieved. Do not drop the new habits you are forming the minute you achieve your goal. Have a maintenance plan in place. If you slip, get back on the horse, and keep going. There is potential for permanent self-sustainable change if you keep reminding yourself that you can do it. Do not let yourself off the hook. Keep your change team in place and know you are in it for the long haul.

## 36) The status quo can be fatal

My associate Sandra Miko's husband, Josef Miko, is an engineering manager at Bosch. He sent me these reflections about change, and they are perfect for this chapter.

*Sticking to what you know and not being willing to experience new approaches can be fatal. I remember when I used to work for a family-owned company. They had started a venture in a different country with very promising possibilities, yet they were unwilling to change and adapt to this new environment. Their approach was to do things the same way they were done in the past. Unfortunately, the past was different and these models proved not to work in the new environment. Consequently, the venture turned out to be an expensive failure and disappointment.*

*No matter if we are living a wealthy or poor life, we may get bored and wish that things were different. There are many people that seem happy with the status quo, but my experience is that in fact most of those people are afraid to change because of uncertainty. To me, this does not sound like a long-term satisfying situation. Does it to you? To keep life interesting, we all need challenges and changes. It's mastering new challenges that keeps us growing and enjoying life.*

*Your accomplishments are what make you grow as a person and increases your confidence. How does that work? How can changes make you grow? Well, if you have mastered certain challenges, then this knowledge of, "I can do this" makes you less afraid of upcoming challenges.*

*Remember everything around you is not static, but in flow. Everyday things are changing a little bit around you. Be it a new driving route to work because of road construction, a different structure in your work environment, or your partner doing something differently. If you embrace these small and large changes, you can try to adapt and make the best of the situation(s).*

Remember CANI, constant and never-ending improvement, means there is no being static, you are always either going forward or going backward. And what have we decided to do? Go forward.

Here are a few quotes about change that support this chapter beautifully:

> *Be the change you want to see in the world.—Mahatma Gandhi*

> *Change is the essence of life. Be willing to surrender what you are for what you could become.—Reinhold Niebuhr*

*If you don't create change, change will
create you.—Unknown*

*When you're finished changing, you're
finished.—Benjamin Franklin*

*If you will change, everything will
change for you.—Jim Rohn*

## Art Van One Percenter: Kevin Gilfillan, Vice President of Sales

Mr. Black Friday, Kevin Gilfillan, wrote his story about changing the game in *Maximum Pumptitude* (Chapter 13, "Black Friday 2009"). Since that time, we have broken countless sales records and had more fun in the process. His focus is never-ending self-development and helping others grow. Enjoy his story—it is a true process of change.

Kevin Gilfillan is a 35-year retail veteran, 30 of those years have been with Art Van Furniture. Kevin has held positions in all areas of retail including stock clerk, maintenance, delivery, service, sales, store management, and corporate leadership.

Since his promotion to vice president of sales in early 2008, Kevin has led the Art Van Furniture sales organization to great success, breaking multiple company single-day sales records, product sales records, and sales event records, including four consecutive Black Friday sales records.

# Embrace change

I had the good fortune of being raised by two amazing parents who taught me the disciplines of commitment and hard work. So I began my working life working hard, and it paid off. After I joined the Art Van team, I quickly climbed the ladder and at the young age of 32, I became store manager of one of the largest Art Van Furniture stores.

A few years later I found myself stagnant. I had become comfortable in my place and my growth had stopped. Hard work had gotten me to where I was, hard work was keeping me in my position, but that was as far as hard work was going to get me.

I attended a seminar called "The Art of Exceptional Living" by Jim Rohn, and was totally inspired. My excitement lasted all of a couple of months, and soon I found myself right back where I was before the seminar. I had done nothing with the learning I received, I took no new actions, I changed nothing and so nothing changed for me. Why would anything change? A seminar is not a magic pill, it's only a start.

But good fortune was watching out for me. I was able to attend the very same seminar a year later; this time, something clicked in me. I realized I had wasted a year by not taking any action, by not changing my life or my habits. Jim's message hit me square between the eyes, especially these two statements: "If you will change, everything will change for you" and "Learn to work harder on yourself than you do on the job. If you work hard on the job you'll make a living. If you'll work harder on yourself, you will make a fortune." Once these statements were ingrained in my head, my life began to grow again.

I changed; I took action to make myself better than I was. I didn't just read books, I studied them. I would read the same book over and over so that the teachings became a part of me.

GARY.
I APPRECIATE YOU MOAS THAN
YOU will EVER KNOW.

135

The best way to embrace change is to change yourself every day. You can't get comfortable or you'll become obsolete. Life is change. Change is constant. We must be open to change, greet it with a smile and say *I look forward to change*.

So what's the end of the story? Well, two years after attending my second chance seminar and working hard on myself, I was promoted to regional sales director. Continuing my self-education, I was then promoted to my current position of vice president of sales. I'm still growing and learning, so there's no end to my story. I will not become obsolete. **If you will change, everything will change for you**.

# — Chapter 8 —

# HAVE SOMETHING TO FIGHT FOR

*If opportunity doesn't knock,*
*build a door.—Milton Berle*

It's important to have something to fight for. People succumb to mediocrity because excellence is hard. It requires extreme motivation. People are at their best when they are fighting for something meaningful to them, their family, their community or their country. The moment there is a wolf at the door threatening home or family, we find another level of resourcefulness and commitment.

We need to consciously find things worth fighting for rather than just cruising along the highway of life until we run out of fuel. We must see the consequences of inaction as a reason for taking action. If you don't have anything to fight for, it's impossible to win.

## 37) Donna becomes a CEO

*If you want to go fast, go alone.*
*If you want to go far, go together.*
*—African proverb*

Though I took credit for that quote in Chapter 7 of *Maximum Pumptitude*, it's actually an African proverb I once heard and instantly integrated into my own personal philosophy.

My wife Donna has done more than her share of inspiring others, which you heard in Chapter 3 (#15) of *Maximum Pumptitude*. However, she never inspired me more than she has done since she took over my Life Chest project as the CEO of our company, Life2000.

I'll go into more details in Chapter 11, but now let me just tell you that Donna is definitely on an inspirational mission, and I am so proud to be watching this take place the way it has. It's all because of something I believe in deeply. When you surround yourself with people who have the same principles and beliefs as you, you will see everyone excel. There really is no easy route; life takes strong actions, true faith, and remarkable tenacity to make things happen. Being first, being humble, and getting stuff done goes miles.

Doing things alone, you can accomplish a lot; doing things together as a team, you can literally change the world in which you live. I am convinced this Life Chest project is going to change the way people think about what they do every day, how they do it and how they are going to be remembered for what they do. It will bring people closer to their past and make them more engaged in their daily activities, and it will get them planning to make their futures worthy. With Donna's help and focus, something as simple as a Life Chest is becoming a movement that will have all of us thinking, "What am I going to be leaving behind?"

She's gone from working from planes, her car and the garage, to a great little office and showroom with a terrific address. She has an eager young executive assistant, Julie, who seems to have adopted Donna's enthusiasm and optimism for the project. The Life Chest team, which includes our daughter Ashley, is meeting people who have done amazing things in their lives. Every single day, new exciting opportunities arise and Donna keeps recognizing them, addressing them, and putting them into action. The Life Chest team is convinced that what they are working so hard on today is going to be responsible for the preservation of the stories and actions of remarkable people everywhere.

What she has been able to accomplish over such a short period of time has a lot of people talking. They are amazed at the transition and the speed at which it has taken place. What do I think? I think that if you surround yourself with successful people, you believe in the power of AND. If you really, really, really want to do something, you will.

## 38) Pick what swords to die on

It's all about understanding what's important versus what's not. As Steve Jobs said, "We say no to the things that don't count so that we can yes to things that do." There is no faster way to become frustrated and fatigued than being upset about things that are not important. We all have finite amounts of physical and mental capital. It's a sin to waste it on things that don't matter. It also demoralizes your colleagues and community, and disturbs their wellbeing and focus.

Leaders need to constantly be thinking about the big picture and what really matters. People usually major in minor things because of their ego. Sometimes, **we must be willing to go along to get along**.

If one falls on every sword, it's like death by a thousand paper cuts. It's not the boulder that kills you; it's the pebble in your shoe. The small issues will drive you insane if you let them.

I often have to remind members of our leadership team that if they keep dying on every sword, they're usually dead by 10:00 a.m. It's far better to outlive the day.

## 39) Thinking big

You met Kevin Gilfillan in the one percenter story at the end of Chapter 7. Let's hear more from him now about thinking big and having a vision:

*Without vision, you are sure to go nowhere. If you don't have a dream or vision for your life, then you're not really going to reach your fullest potential. Maybe at one time you had a dream, but you went through some disappointments or setbacks. Things didn't turn out the way you planned. But here's a key reminder: Just because it didn't work out the way you had it planned doesn't mean that your dream is dead.*

*You cannot allow one disappointment, or even a series of disappointments, convince you that your dream is over. It's time to dig in your heels and hold onto the promises in your heart. Stir up those dreams today and watch what happens!*

*You can do amazing things! You can accomplish amazing goals! But you have to have a clear vision of your goals and dreams and then believe!*

*Goal setting or, as I like to call it, dream planning, is simple if you think of it like taking a vacation.*

*First, decide where you want to go. Be specific.*

*Second, decide when you want to go. You must put a date on it.*

*Third, figure out how you're going to get there. Start building your plan.*

*You can go anywhere you decide to go. You can become anyone you decide to become. You just need to think big and dream.*

## 40) No dumptitude

In *Pumptitude* (Chapter 7, #43), we shared that you want to avoid energy vampires at all costs. In his book *The Energy Bus*, John Gordon describes energy vampires in great detail. He indicated that all of us, at times, will come across people of great negativity who suck the life out of an event, a meeting, or any general occasion. In *Maximum Pumptitude* (Chapter 3, #10), we elaborated on this concept and explained that in addition to energy vampires, you should look to avoid people who suffer from grumptitude, or high levels of grumpiness. Well, now we're introducing to you the concept of dumptitude.

When certain people approach you, you can hear the truck coming with them. Just like the garbage trucks on the street, backing up as they get ready to dump their load, you'll hear, "Beep, beep, beep," as these people arrive. Get ready for the garbage!

These people pull up their trucks, figuratively speaking, and dump out everything that's bothering them. When this happens, your natural instinct is to do one of two things. One, you start upping them in terms of all the bad things that are happening to you, saying something like, "You think you've got problems, listen to this!" Or two, by the time they've dumped their entire load on you, you're so depressed that it's hard to go on with the rest of your day.

My advice when somebody pulls up, puts their truck in reverse, and starts to beep is no different than how we handle the energy vampires, and no different than how we handle grumptitude. Avoid the dumptituders! This is not for us.

Here's a real-life example of dumptitude in action. My mother often tells me that she received several phone calls from friends and relatives through the course of one day. It takes no time for her to hear the beeping sound of them backing their trucks up to her so they can dump their garbage. Imagine somebody thinking that it's okay to dump their garbage on someone else! What my mother reminds me is that when I call her, I'm like an antidote to the dumptitude. I call with enthusiasm, excitement about what I'm doing, what I'm accomplishing, and the great things that are coming into my life. By doing so, my goal is to put her back on track in a positive way herself because nobody deserves to be a dumped on with garbage from everyone else.

My associate and executive assistant Sandra Miko has these further thoughts to share about the concept of no dumptitude:

*I have worked with many people who did not like their jobs; all I heard was complaining, day in and day out. I was actually friends with a few complainers, which made me a complainer. Believe it or not, I was a very good complainer—just for a short time. Remember the movie Invasion of the Body Snatchers? Well I was almost taken by the Invasion of the Complainers! Thank goodness, in the nick of time, I was able to pull myself away from the Complainer's Club! Every day, I am so thankful that I did not let the complainers overpower me.*

*These types of people would complain about everything—not being promoted, not being asked to be on special projects, etc. Well, I wonder why they weren't chosen?*

*If you keep on going along in life without learning, improving or enjoying your career, ultimately, you will turn into a very unhappy person. When you are unhappy with your job, it affects your personal life. Thus, you will be unhappy with your entire life and no one will want to be a part of it.*

*Don't let this happen! It is so much better being happy. If you're not happy in your current position, you better find out what would make you happy and do something about it. How do you do this? Change!*

## Attitudes are contagious. Is yours worth catching?

The greatest source of unhappiness is self-unhappiness. Unhappiness comes from the inside—so does happiness. **We are the authors of our own drama**.

# 41) The power of inspiration

In his book *Start With Why*, author Simon Sinek enlightens us about what he calls the Golden Circle. Imagine a circle with the word "Why" inside. Then picture a larger circle around that one, with the word "How" inside. Finally, imagine an even larger third circle around that one, labeled with the word, "What."

These circles represent the what, how and why as to how we behave and function. In the book, Sinek explains that while most of us can easily describe *what* we do in life, and even *how* we do it, things get fuzzy when it comes to the *why*.

He says that's why it isn't about making money (that's a result); it's about what drives you to get out of bed in the morning. What belief do you stand behind and stand up for?

*[handwritten: You the best — Thnks for all yey support]*

Let's get another perspective on internal motivation from Art Van Vice President of Strategic Development Steve Glucksman who writes:

What motivates me? After pondering the question, I realized it really comes down to just three things:

1. *Success. I like to add value and win. I want to leave things better than the way I found them, whether at work or at home. If I fail, I try and try again—I am a strong believer in persistence.*

2. *Fear. I am afraid of failure and of letting down my family, team, or myself. That is certainly a motivator. I don't want to be the guy to strike out with bases loaded in the bottom of the ninth. I may not hit the home run, either, but I can do everything in my power to keep the game going.*

3. *Desire. Like that old U.S. Army advertisement promised, I want to be all I can be. I am motivated to have more, whether those are material or non-material things. I think we all want to love/be loved more, be smarter, be healthier, be more spiritual, be better off professionally, personally and financially, and be able to give more back.*

Simon Sinek's *The Golden Circle* is about changing the paradigm so that each of us starts with the why and looks at our lives from the center out instead of from the outside in.

He writes about how leaders who focus on the why move from manipulating others to inspiring them. We can see examples of this kind of leadership throughout history in leaders who motivated the people around them to work harder and smarter than they ever did before. They inspired people to act versus just talk. They inspired people to take action, versus being spectators. Remember that *I-Pump*—internal pumptitude—starts first within.

As Ken Kesey remarked, you can count the number of seeds in an apple, but you can't count the number of apples in the seed. You can always tell where the process starts but you can

David Van – Art Van VP of Merchandising, Sheilah P. Clay – Neighborhood Service Organization,
Susan Goodell – Forgotten Harvest, Sheri Mark – North Star Reach,
Chuck Saur – Conductive Learning Center, Cecilia Chesney – Big Brothers Big Sisters
of Northwestern Michigan and Kim Yost – Art Van CEO

never tell where the process ends. A powerful WHY starts the process. It's like the seed in the apple. Every action is like an apple, and every action is a cause set in motion.

For the last three years in a row, Art Van has held a special ceremony to honor five high achievers—one percenters who run five non-profit charity organizations in Michigan. I recently had the good fortune to be a speaker during this year's event. After the five honorees had received their awards and a sizable cash donation to each of their charities, I had the opportunity to sum up and speak about these inspiring individuals.

I chose three words to focus on in my speech: *inspire, grow* and *more*. (If you remember, these are Mike Lipkin's three favorite words from Chapter 1, #2.)

I pointed out the many ways that these special honorees understood and used these three words to influence and change others beyond belief; how they inspired everyone around them to think and achieve beyond the norm; how they challenged all they came in contact with to grow in every aspect of their lives, push endless boundaries of what they believed they could accomplish, and to become so much more than they were before. When you *inspire* others to *grow*, it always leads to *more*.

For years, I have tried to be a great inspiration to others, and I'd like to share the top nine mental reminders and behaviors that I use to inspire myself, and the top six behaviors I use to inspire others.

## Myself

1. Constant self-talk that if they can do it, I can do it.

2. Reminding myself of the amount of work that my coaches and mentors have done on me over the years and that I won't disappoint their expectations of me.

3. Trying always to positively impress my family, my wife, my daughter, and my colleagues.

4. Always imagining what my role models, or the people I most envy, would do if they were in my situation.

5. Focusing on the marathon, not the sprint, so that I won't have to lose all that I have become.

6. Always giving myself some form of a reward at the end of a great accomplishment.

7. When I get closer to the finish line, I don't want to have any regrets that I could have become much more than I ended up becoming. (Remember the definition of hell from *Maximum Pumptitude*, Chapter 10, #60?)

8. Daily rituals of 60 minutes of I-Pump exercise (the 23-hour day) and my weekly eighth day (Schmonday).

9. Being inspired when I see my coaching and mentoring pay off with one of my young protégés doing amazingly well.

## Others

1. I aspire to be the very best role model.

2. I tell stories constantly as a form of teaching, using both analogies and metaphors to make my points.

3. I am constantly challenging people to become more than even what they see in themselves.

4. I encourage people to focus on the task at hand so that they can truly benefit from the results they have achieved.

5. I give people empowerment, autonomy and the encouragement to risk failure.

6. The most powerful inspiration that I can give is trust.

I hope you enjoyed this honest and transparent look at how I inspire myself and others. It's truly a big part of my DNA. Next, get ready to realize why living on an island all alone will leave you just that, all alone. We one percenters live to be with others and enjoy the relationships we continue to have and build on.

# One Percenter: Colin Donnelly, Husband and Father

I'm excited to introduce a dear friend and past colleague. Working alongside Colin Donnelly at The Brick for over 10 years, I watched his success and reinvention in amazement. Few people know this, but Colin was the originator of giving away free televisions with sofa living room packages. Over the years, every North American furniture retailer has adopted that child (idea), and has sold hundreds of thousands of living room packages with those free TVs. I still remember the day when Colin, Bill Comrie and I were sitting in a meeting and the idea was born. Enjoy his story, as I've enjoyed watching his life continue to grow.

||||||||||||||||||||||||||||||||||||||||||||||||||||||||||||||||||||||||||||||||||||||||||||||||

Colin Donnelly joined Dorel Asia in Jan 2006. In the very short years since, we have vaulted Dorel Asia into becoming a dominant upholstery source for industry giants including Walmart, Target, Sam's Club, Kmart, Sears and more. Our success is a result of creating a brand that focuses on design, quality and engineering while still boasting the most competitive pricing.

||||||||||||||||||||||||||||||||||||||||||||||||||||||||||||||||||||||||||||||||||||||||||||||||

I was honored that Kim wanted me to share what keeps me driven, focused, motivated and inspired, plus how I build a personal and business brand.

I am grateful, very grateful, for everything I have. I grew up poor, moving 10 times in 10 years because rent money wasn't easy. My mother did an amazing job hiding her stress and kept our family full of love and light. Early in my teen years, I defined who I was; I saw the person that I wanted to be become. This was the start of my brand.

We are all motivated differently. I love to turn up the volume on life's dial. Why keep that drive alive? Why get up before 6:00 a.m. when I could sleep a few extra hours? My eyes are barely open in the morning, and I'm reaching to unplug my iPhone so that I can see the first wave of emails. It's easy, when you love what you do.

Love is the foundation for everything. Love your job, love your family and friends, love life. Our time here is very short, so choose your battles. Do not attach other people's pain or anger to your own being. Each day is such a gift, so choose to celebrate life. Charge on and enjoy the people that fill your space each day.

Can you imagine that the space between two objects is not just air, but a complex mail system that captures your thoughts and transcends them to the universe to become processed? Your thoughts are real, so visualize and believe. If you realized how powerful your thoughts were, you would never think a negative thought again. Train your mind to find the positive in everything you do, the things you see and the people that you meet. Creative expression, thoughts and ideas need positive energy. *Negative energy will stop the flow of creative ideas*.

Motivation comes automatically when you have a desire for that winning feeling. To sell something that you developed, created, designed or negotiated. We all love the feeling of success, like when the puck slides past the goalie and finds its way into the net. It's a great feeling every time. Jack Welch recognized that all successes should be celebrated, even the small ones. This recognition motivates everyone. It motivates me to watch my peers succeed. It motivates me to see successful people still working in their 80s. They do it because they want to, not because they have to. Do something that you love and you will become successful. Life is a celebration.

# — Chapter 9 —

# **RELATIONSHIPS**

*If civilization is to survive, we must cultivate the science of human relationships - the ability of all peoples, of all kinds, to live together, in the same world at peace.—Franklin D. Roosevelt*

In Chapter 3, #16, I talked about personality tests that help you understand and communicate better with others. We all need to be acutely aware of how we're thinking and acting, and the impact we're having on others.

Whenever two people come together, there are really six people meeting—there is who we really are, who we think we are, and who the other person thinks we are. So those are the first three people. Then there is the real other person, who the person thinks they are, and who we think that person is. That's why communication is so complex, and that's why clear communication is so important.

## 42) Mentorship

*The best teachers are those who show you where to look, but don't tell you what to see.—Alexandra K. Trenfor*

People need to take the time to mentor others. This is not a chore, it's a privilege. It's an obligation for anyone who has benefited from the wisdom of others. It's about paying it forward. We can choose others that we want to mentor and sometimes they will choose us. It's a huge compliment to be asked by someone to be their mentor, but we shouldn't wait to be asked, we should offer.

Those who mentor others learn from their "mentees" as well. The more we coach others, the more focused we become. We also build the currency of reciprocation that will pay huge dividends over time. We need to find the time to do it because there is no better investment of our time.

In *Twelfth Night*, Shakespeare wrote, "Be not afraid of greatness. Some are born great, some achieve greatness, and others have greatness thrust upon them." We are born with certain talents that automatically evolve. Then we have to choose mentors that help us achieve levels of excellence. We find mentors by identifying candidates and asking for their mentorship. We become what we teach and what we are taught. No matter how old we are, we should all have people that we can go to on a regular basis. Even Tiger Woods has a coach. Champions and mentors go together.

## 43) Moment of pleasure, lifelong of misery

Many of us have real challenges in maintaining and growing our personal relationships with the ones we love. For those who are in a marriage or other significant relationship, our commitment to being faithful can get tested. I got the best advice on this topic years ago from an early mentor, Mr. Peter Koel.

When I was 26 years old, I was a furniture buyer working for the Woodwards department store. Mr. Koel and I were on a trip to Europe, specifically Milan, Italy. One night, after a long day at the furniture show, Peter and I went out for dinner and ended up at the hotel bar for a late nightcap. Two amazingly beautiful women came over to our table, asked if they could sit down, and asked if we would buy them a bottle of champagne. Mr. Koel declined the offer, and, when they left, he gave the best advice for a married young traveler. He told me those girls did not just want conversation. Furthermore, the bottle of champagne they wanted to order would have cost us over $800. Then he said, "Remember this, Kim. A moment of pleasure, a lifelong of misery."

Over the years, I've witnessed several married or committed individuals getting involved with someone outside of that committed relationship, especially when on business trips a long way from home. Several of these episodes resulted in disasters in their marriage and relationships. So if you are in a relationship and ever find yourself tested, remember Mr. Koel's sound advice.

## 44) It's only feedback

In my first book, *Pumptitude* (Chapter 10, #55), I encouraged you to seek out feedback as a way to grow and take your game to the next level. I shared a powerful lesson from Art Van Elslander about how long after we're finished school, we continue to get report cards about how we're doing in all areas of life.

Then in the introduction to Chapter 7 in *Maximum Pumptitude*, I point out that sometimes the most meaningful feedback comes from the people who irritate us.

People show how we're doing in our relationships by voting with their feet. Are we someone they want to spend time with? Are they turning towards us or away from us?

I have been so encouraged by the number of people who are walking towards me to let me know about the positive impact my work is having on their lives. This has been hugely rewarding for me.

It's all about giving people the right combination of information and inspiration that enables them to play at their personal best. Whether you are giving positive feedback or constructive feedback, you should never underestimate the power of even a single sentence on someone else's life.

## 45) Gratitude

Throughout this series, we've talked about pumptitude, grumptitude and dumptitude. Now let's talk about gratitude.

Internal pumptitude comes from an acute level of thankfulness for the abundance of opportunity and freedom that we have in North America. We need to be thankful for friends, family and health. We should focus on what we have versus what we don't have. In fact, whatever we take for granted gets taken away. When people are miserable, all they need to do is focus specifically on their blessings and they can become magnificent. You can't be a one percenter if you're not grateful.

## 46) That's brilliant

Later in this book (Chapter 10, #54), you will learn about the art of adopting and building on other people's ideas. The truth is, however, that not every idea you come across is going to be worth adopting.

"That's brilliant!" is something we all want to hear when we present a new idea. But this is a precious statement and should not be delivered lightly. Years ago, I started sharing a humorous but important reminder with people that it's not until an idea has been acted upon and executed that it becomes a brilliant.

I'd say, "That's a brill! If you do something about it, you get the back end." At the office, we constantly remind each other that many great brills can become brilliant when acted upon and executed. So don't be too anxious to give out a "That's brilliant!" for just an idea. By giving out "brills" instead of "brilliants," you will constantly remind people that an idea might sound impressive, but without the follow through, without the completion and implementation of the idea, it's just a great thought.

# 47) A legacy like no other—even a coffin can inspire creativity

I have been sharing this story about my young friend David Scofield for years. We were friends from the first day we met at school in Grade 9; he became "Scony" moments later. He had moved from Montreal, Quebec, to Vancouver, British Columbia, which is almost entirely across our country. His big smile and willingness to share everything that he had were two of his best personal qualities. David was incredibly talented and driven.

David also gave me my first and only tattoo—a crude and very painful design that he carried out with two sharp sewing needles, 2.5-inches long, criss-crossed at the top and tied to the end of a pencil. Oh, there was blood everywhere—it was absolutely barbaric! I still remember screaming from the pain.

At the age of 13, I started my second business (my first business at the age of 11 was building plastic models and selling them to stores), making and selling black light posters and hookah pipes. David worked in this business. His role on our team was to dry the posters after they had been inked and roll them into individual plastic wrappers.

After several years of friendship and hundreds of posters and hookah pipe sales later, David died suddenly at the age of 17. He got into his white MG sports car late one night after drinking way too much, drove into a tree, and killed himself. This was my first tragic loss of anyone I truly cared for. His parents were going through a divorce at the time, which made his death even harder.

Both of David's parents were challenged financially and could not afford a proper burial, so all his friends were asked to contribute. I was making a modest living at the time, working in the back stockroom of Woodwards department store, so things were tight for me as well. David's death was devastating to me and our group of friends, and I really wanted to help.

One day while the funeral preparations were being developed, I was taking a large Braemar furniture curio cabinet out of the stockroom onto the showroom floor. It struck me that this curio cabinet would make a great coffin. With my 15 percent employee discount and free delivery, it would be $119—more than $2,000 less than what the funeral home wanted for a traditional coffin.

Now, the funeral home did need a little convincing to bury Scony in the curio cabinet. It took six of us guys (all over 200 pounds each) making a personal visit to convince them, but they finally agreed.

During the funeral, I sat in the second row from the front with Scony's aunt. We played his favorite song by The Moody Blues, "Nights in White Satin," and there he lay, inside this curio cabinet with its oak finish, beveled-glass side, and mirrored back with piano light kit. His aunt said to me that the coffin must be a new design, because she could see him through the sides of the glass, "from his toes to his nose." I responded back by saying, "Nothing but the best for my friend Scony!"

The legacy we gave Scony was like no other. He is probably the only human ever in history to be buried in a furniture curio display cabinet.

I have lost several other loved ones since Scony's death, including my adopted father in the fall of 2012. I am constantly reminded that we need to cherish every day that we are with our loved ones because all we can be certain of is that we don't know what tomorrow brings. So spend time with your loved ones and tell them you love them. Do it today. Do it now.

## One Percenter: Dennis W. Archer, President & CEO of Ignition Media Group (IMG)

I remember to this day, the first time I met Mr. Star Power, Dennis Archer. His presence in a room is electrifying. His charisma and ability to connect with everybody around him makes him the true one percenter that he is. In just a few short years of knowing Dennis, he's added tremendous value to my life, both personally and professionally. I am so pleased to include him in this book. Ladies and gentlemen, Mr. Relationship Builder, Dennis Archer!

||||||||||||||||||||||||||||||||||||||||||||||||||||||||||||||||||||||||||||||||||||||||||||||||||||||||||||||

 An attorney by trade, Dennis W. Archer, Jr. is the founding partner and president of Archer Corporate Services (ACS;) a founding principal of Hamilton Woodlynne Publishing, which publishes *Ambassador*, and the president & CEO of Ignition Media Group (IMG). Leveraging his background in marketing and advertising, Archer has built a portfolio of companies, each a leader in its respective field.

Archer serves on the boards of the Detroit Regional Chamber, the Jalen Rose Leadership Academy, the Michigan Black Chamber of Commerce, and the Dennis W. Archer Foundation. He lives in Detroit with his wife, Judge Roberta Cheryl Archer, and their two sons, Dennis Wayne Archer, III (Trey) and Chase Alexander Archer.

||||||||||||||||||||||||||||||||||||||||||||||||||||||||||||||||||||||||||||||||||||||||||||||||||||||||||||||

I am honored that Kim, whom I consider a friend and mentor, invited me to be a part of this project. I have benefitted from Kim's advice, such as *Pumptitude*'s suggestion to write down five things I want to accomplish every day. When I do this, I am far more productive.

My inclusion in a chapter devoted to relationships is particularly fitting as many of my professional experiences and accomplishments can be traced directly to a preexisting relationship. Given this recognition, I often urge others to value each introduction, to develop a tool for tracking and maintaining relationships (technology makes this much easier), and to entertain requests for helping others even when the payoff is not immediately apparent.

If business success is the ultimate goal, it certainly goes without saying that relationships are only part of this overall equation:

Preparedness (tools) + Opportunity (relationships) = Luck (success)

Certainly, you cannot possibly be prepared for every opportunity that crosses your path. However, you can prepare yourself to be able to analyze the merit of opportunities that are presented to you.

Although I studied law as opposed to business, it was my legal education that equipped me with tools to analyze opportunities and to selectively pursue those that, through luck and relationships, "fell into my lap."

In high school, Brad Keywell and I played on opposing tennis teams. We both went to Michigan for undergrad and law school, where we began exploring business opportunities. In 2003, Brad called me to discuss a joint venture. We went to dinner, we hit it off, we started a business, and, 10 years later, we celebrated our highest revenue year at ACS. We provide world-class marketing services to GM, P&G, J&J, Michelin and others. Brad is my partner.

This is just one example of how my life has been in large part influenced by the people I have met along my life's journey.

I have 8,000 contacts in my Blackberry, relationships that I have cultivated over time. In many ways, those contacts and the relationships we have formed, tell my life's story.

# — Chapter 10 —

# UNCOMMON LEADERSHIP

*If your actions inspire others to
dream more, learn more, do more and
become more, you are a leader.*
*—John Quincy Adams*

In this chapter, I will share with you my years of learning and the experiences that have shaped my uncommon leadership behaviors. I have always approached my leadership style with great urgency and focus. Two of my key disciplines have been thinking there is a wolf at the door, even when there may not be, and staying focused on the things that really count, especially in these times of never-ending changes.

I want to share my secrets with you of running a large, rapidly-evolving, and complex organization. How do I do it? How do I successfully and constantly enroll people in my causes?

## 48) Focus—kill King Darius

One of the strongest behaviors that a one percenter and top-grade leader needs is the ability to stay focused. When so many distractions are coming at us, from so many different directions, it's that ability to stay on track with laser focus that separates the ultimate achievers. Here's a story that I have told over the past years to many leadership teams. I use it to spell out how terrifically successful you and your team can be if you can stay focused on a single thought, goal, or project.

Now this story has some biblical references, but as I've told it so many times, I've taken the liberty of simplifying it for the purpose of being able to teach the concept of the power of single-minded focus.

Imagine in your mind's eye two amazing leaders in biblical times engaged in a battle like no other. One leader has consolidated one million troops from several countries all over the Middle East. The one million troops have an allegiance to King Darius and have come to this battle to conquer their adversary, an army of only one thousand troops led by King David. King David has a profound reputation for defeating other adversaries, time after time, against phenomenal odds.

Imagine, on one side of this major battleground, you have a million troops, and perched on top of the hill above them is the tent of King Darius. Across from the million troops, you have King David with his thousand troops. Both leaders are positioned to commence a battle the following morning at 8:00 a.m.—one million to one thousand.

The night before the big battle, King David's 10 sergeants, each the leader of 100 troops, came to his tent, quite worried and arguably stressed. They asked what their battle plan was given the odds of one million to a thousand. King David indicated that he would give them their plan at 7:45 a.m., and that they should rest up and get a good night's sleep because the following day they would be victorious. I'm sure most of them didn't get much sleep at all.

The following morning, King David kept his word and gave his troops their battle plan, shortly before 8:00 a.m. on the day of the big battle. The plan was not to kill one million soldiers, but to kill just one—King Darius. They asked for more details, but King David's orders were simply, "Kill King Darius."

Here's what happened next: King David's one thousand soldiers lined up in a narrow column, and started marching directly towards the tent of King Darius. Since they knew their goal was not to kill anyone except King Darius, they marched steadily and quickly through the massive crowd of King Darius's soldiers. Their narrow line was pointed almost like a spear.

Their singleness of focus rendered the million soldiers useless, since, with the exception of the small group that were directly in front of and beside them, King David's soldiers were not engaging in battle with them. If you're not trying to kill anyone, just trying to get by them, you can move much faster.

If King David's troops had faced their opponents spread out and head on, you can be sure the battle would have been over almost as soon as it began. As it was, by 10:00 a.m., King David's troops were about halfway to the tent of King Darius. By noon, they were three-quarters of the way there. Seeing their approach, King Darius panicked, "They're coming to my tent! They're coming to kill me!" He retreated and fled only to be killed by his own men for retreating. By early afternoon, King David's troops had reached the tent of King Darius and knocked down his flag, indicating to the million troops that King Darius's tent had fallen. The million troops immediately realized that King David had won another unbelievable battle, and so they fled because their allegiance was tied to one man, and one man only, King Darius.

The success of this battle was tied to its simplicity, the single-minded focus of the one thousand troops led by King David, and their never-ending quest to stay focused on their goal. By doing so, they achieved overwhelming results. So can you. The genius of King David's plan was that he did not focus on a mile wide and an inch deep. He focused on a mile deep and an inch wide.

Even when you face insurmountable odds like King David, if you've got a plan that people can buy into, and you can stay focused on that plan, you will achieve remarkable things. When you think of focus and its benefits to you and your team, think of these five words:

**F**antastic

**O**ptimism

**C**ommunication

**U**nity

**S**uccess

## 49) Level 5 leader—work hard on your team and you can make history

Author, speaker and consultant Jim Collins describes the importance of being a Level 5 leader versus a Level 4 leader. Simply stated, a Level 4 leader suffering from high levels of narcissism and showmanship, clearly indicates to everyone that it's all about them. History has proven that Level 4 leaders can make a big difference and have positive impact on a team or an organization, but the downside is that when they leave, or if anything negative happens to them, their organizations typically fail because everything was all about that one person.

On the other hand, a Level 5 leader displays behavior that's consistent with team building. Everything is always about the team and building the people around the Level 5 leader. The goal of a Level 5 leader is that the organization will continue to grow and prosper without them because of its deep talent pool. It's never about them; it's always about everybody else.

At the end of Chapter 7, one percenter Kevin Gilfillan quoted Jim Rohn: "If you work hard on the job you'll make a living. If you'll work harder on yourself, you will make a fortune." To this I would add, "And if you work on your team, you can make history!"

I have a dear friend named Simon Kaplan who is in his 80s. He fought in World War II and liberated several European countries in that epic conflict. When World War II ended, he moved to New Jersey and started a furniture company. Mr. Kaplan has been developing his business, Value City Furniture, for over five decades, and he illustrates the best I've ever seen in Level 5 leadership. What I've come to know about Simon is that it's always about his team, always about the people that have made him the success he is.

As I wrote in *Maximum Pumptitude* (Chapter 3, #16), when you put the spotlight on others, it shines twice as brightly upon you. This is clearly the case with Simon. Another amazing thing that Simon did at the end of WWII was to hire several veterans into his business right from the start, both in sales and in management.

Kim Yost, Donna Yost, Simon Kaplan and Ashley Yost

Recently, Simon sent me a book called *Beyond Band of Brothers: The War Memories of Major Dick Winters*. In Simon's view, this book includes some learning about Level 5 leadership. Its 10 leadership behaviors, referred to as leadership at the point of a bayonet, are ones that Simon has successfully demonstrated for years.

I'd like to call out four of these behaviors and show how they tie into the concepts we've been sharing in this Pumptitude series.

For example, the third principle, "Stay in top physical shape," is something I wrote about in *Pumptitude*, Chapter 7, #42, when I encouraged you to live a 23-hour day by dedicating one "power hour" every day for exercise. In Chapter 2 of *Maximum Pumptitude*, I shared the surprising strategy of the power nap and how that contributes to your physical and mental stamina.

Finally, in Chapter 5, #23 of this book, I suggested that the hardest part of getting in your daily exercise might just be getting started. So just put on your shorts and go, and you are guaranteed to see a huge return on your investment.

The sixth principle of leadership at the point of a bayonet is to anticipate problems and prepare to overcome obstacles. In military terms, Winters says, "Don't wait until you get to the top of the ridge and then make up your mind." I also urge you to move quickly when you get a new idea, or when you need to make a decision, as I discussed in lesson #37 ("Cut your losses") of *Maximum Pumptitude*. We must have the courage to get out of a bad situation and move on to the next challenge. Never procrastinate!

In Principle #7, Winters advises leaders to remain humble. "Don't worry about who receives the credit. Never let power or authority go to your head." Humility is one of three key qualities I identified in *Maximum Pumptitude* (Chapter 3, #16, "Stay smart, hungry and humble") that I look for in prospective team members and also in myself.

Let's look at one more principle from *Beyond Band of Brothers*. The eighth principle invites you to take a moment of self-reflection, time to look at yourself in the mirror every night and ask yourself if you did your best. I identified this kind of self-assessment as one of the four key learning points in Stage 2 of life (*Maximum Pumptitude*, Chapter 11, #64), which is the education phase between ages 17 and 27. It's a practice I recommend no matter what stage you're at, and that's why it was also one of the first 10 lessons I shared in *Pumptitude* (Chapter 1, #9), when I asked you to assess where you are now and where you want to be in the eight main areas of your life.

I tip my hat to Mr. Simon Kaplan, for adopting a leadership style that has proven successful on the battlefield and in business.

## 50) Rusty nails—you cannot make everyone a winner

There are times when we, as leaders, try to take individuals and work with them, coach them, inspire them, and motivate them to be more than who they are and move beyond what they're capable of. Here are two stories that will help you understand that for one percenters and top graders in leadership, you sometimes have to take a different path when it comes to building your team and working with specific people.

Years ago, I was having dinner with my friend, author Brian Tracy, and a few of The Brick's warehouse leaders. Bob Gillespie, one of our VPs of sales, asked Brian how he could get more sales executives who sell more than a million dollars a year. For years, Bob had struggled with recruiting and educating these million-dollar writers. Brian Tracy's response was very simple, "Bob, if you want more million-dollar writers, my suggestion is that you *hire* more million-dollar writers. Because the likelihood is that you're hiring half-a-million-dollar writers, time after time."

It's like hiring a groundhog to climb a tree, Brian explained. No matter what you try, the groundhog won't be able to do it, and all you're going to do is frustrate yourself and the groundhog. If you want a tree climbed, hire a squirrel!

Mr. Art Van Elslander has a story with a similar lesson about trying to make people into something they're not. He told me that for years, he would take different individuals under his wing, people he felt had great promise, but for a variety of reasons could not make the grade in either sales or leadership. Someone told Mr. Van to think of a person like that as a rusty, bent nail. Many leaders have a strong tendency to want to straighten out that nail and polish off that rust; instead, they should just go get a new nail.

When we, as leaders, are building high-performance teams, we must always keep in mind that there will be individuals who will excel, who will reinvent themselves, who will continue to grow, and who will truly benefit from our coaching, but there are others who will stay bent and rusted and never be able to climb a tree. Have the wisdom to know the difference between the two.

## 51) Life of constant motion

Objects in constant movement tend to stay in movement. Negativity cannot stick to you if you're constantly contributing value to others and the world.

We know that one positive contributor to being a one percenter is being busy. They lead active lives, and they have active minds. A one percenter's outward signal is that everything about them is busy. There are no voids in their days, weeks or months. They're constantly planning and achieving, and there's a never-ending cycle of activity. One percenters are always moving; they tend to thrive on busy-ness, and the chair is definitely not their friend.

Get into motion and stay in motion. Once you get that momentum, it's easier to keep it going. The same is true for fitness and exercise. It's far more effective to do 30 minutes of exercise every day for a week, than to do no exercise throughout the week and do hours of strenuous activity on the weekend. These "weekend warriors" often find themselves incapable of doing anything on Monday morning due to their aches and pains. It's easier to maintain a steady level of fitness than to have to constantly get back into it over and over again.

That being said, remember that it's vital to replenish your reserves with recreation and relaxation. All work and no play can burn us out. One is not sustainable without the other, and no one can be extraordinary in your personal and professional life without them both.

It's a paradox, but without rest, you cannot be in constant motion. Motion without rest is burnout. This is the power of the catnap and power naps. It's moments of "mini-hibernation" or moments of recharging. One of the greatest skills that we can master is the ability to catnap on demand because you don't know when you're going to get the next chance to rest and recover.

In Chapter 7 of *Pumptitude* about making energy, I explained the importance of managing your energy so that'll have enough to make a great life. Of course this includes creating a good sleep environment with the right mattress and pillows.

## 52) If you become more, more will be expected of you

*Each success only buys an admission ticket to a more difficult problem.*
*—Henry Kissinger*

During my days at The Brick Group, Bill Comrie and I were embarking on a 10-day trip to South Africa. We were going to start in Cape Town, go through Johannesburg, and, in the last seven days, we would be on safari in Kruger National Park. I was so excited about this trip, I had been preparing for weeks.

One day before our departure, Bill and I were walking down the hallway when he started tossing out several new ideas and initiatives. Each one would take months to implement and would have a significant impact on the company. As he loaded me up with these plans, I was getting more and more stressed.

At this point I was president and CEO, and felt that I was pretty much in charge of controlling all my own activities and to dos. Yet, just one day before this huge 10-day trip, I was getting lambasted with a whole set of new challenges.

I lost it. I said something like, "Well, I'll just cancel my trip. You go to South Africa. I'll stay back and start working on these new initiatives tomorrow." Bill looked at me for a moment, saw how frazzled I was, and pulled me into his office to give me what became a most important lesson.

Bill shared that as you become more, more would be expected of you, and that I should never put a self-imposed ceiling on my capacity. He taught me that my response should have been, "Yes, Bill, these are all great initiatives! We can discuss them when we're on our trip, and plan for starting our work on them when we return." He explained that I could have approached the new activities in a much calmer and controlled fashion.

As part of this unscheduled teaching moment, Bill described someone who was doing this very successfully. As a board member on one of Alberta's largest energy companies, he had been amazed to watch the president and CEO of that company during board meetings. This executive would be thrown suggestions, challenges and demands from all different directions, often when he wasn't expecting them. Yet, this top-performing CEO handled it like a pro. He fully understood that as he became more, more would be expected of him.

From that day on, no matter what is thrown at me and by whom, and no matter how busy or active I am, I can always take on more. I will always figure out how to deal with it, and I do it in a very calm and focused fashion. So the next time you want to break through that glass ceiling that we put on ourselves, remind yourself that if you want to become more, you can be guaranteed that more will be expected of you. Deal with it in a professional and successful manner.

## 53) Readers become leaders, and leaders are readers

As we have spoken countless times about the importance of reading and building a library, I want to remind you that books should be part of your legacy. The books you read and the books that you save all tell a story about who you are, so choose them carefully.

One very helpful resource for choosing the books for your library is an executive book summary service, such as Soundview, the one I told you about in *Maximum Pumptitude* (Chapter 5, #36). Book summaries give you the 20 percent of the book you need to move forward with your learning and growth. Using this service allows me to keep up with several new books every month.

In Appendix B, you will find my current list of Top 100 Books. These are just a few of my favorite books, the ones that have given me inspiration to grow both personally and professionally.

You may want to build your own library using two categories—personal development and business. Your library may also include books related to your hobbies, such as golf, aviation, architecture, etc. Great! But if you ultimately want success, make sure you cover the categories of personal development and business.

In my office, I have a small inventory of books and audio books. I am constantly giving out and sharing books that I believe will help others. In turn, I get two or three books each week from friends and colleagues doing the same. When you become a student of life, be sure to share your great new finds with your colleagues, friends and family. As you keep reading and learning, you'll gravitate towards great knowing and filter that to others through your own unique lens, as I've tried to do in this *Pumptitude* series. Everybody wins when you share knowledge.

Building your own library is one of the most important habits you can develop, and Schmonday is the perfect time to review your library and spend time reading and re-reading the powerful lessons others have captured. Jim Rohn notes that all wealthy, successful entrepreneurs have libraries in their home and their office. So start building your library, one book at a time.

## 54) Become an adoption agency

In several of the companies that I've worked with over the years, I have witnessed that some have a culture of adopting new ideas and others don't. Some workplace cultures and some leaders are only prepared to execute on their own ideas. What I promote throughout our leadership team at Art Van is that if we want to continue to grow, we must be a great *adoption agency*. Consider ideas as children, and, just as people adopt children, we need to adopt someone else's ideas.

I have seen that in companies whose leaders are great adopters of each other's ideas, the company moves quicker and faster in the right direction than those who don't adopt. What I recommend is getting into the habit of adopting other people's ideas and running with them as if they're our own children. If we don't, we'll constantly do the same things or perpetuate our own ideas, which doesn't maximize our performance.

If you only fall in love with your own ideas, it limits your personal and professional growth and success. I applaud and worship anyone who constantly and enthusiastically adopts other people's ideas. Don't forget that you can add value to someone else's idea and give it your own personal touch. It will ultimately then become yours. At the end of the day, become a great adoption agency and look to adopt other people's ideas so that you can contribute to the success of those ideas.

Unfortunately, some good ideas never get traction because the originator cannot persuade others about the greatness of the ideas. When you put your own ideas up for adoption, you must have a great deal of belief and passion as well as the ability to sell your idea in order to get others to adopt. Remember that you cannot get others to do what you are not prepared to do.

If you have an amazing idea and are truly vested in it, remember you've got to sell it as if your life depended on it. I love this saying that Gary Van Elslander, President of Art Van, repeats frequently: "A great idea has many fathers, a bad idea is an orphan."

The lessons of leadership and mentorship can help us all, no matter where and who we are in life, whether we are leaders or whether we aspire to be leaders. I truly appreciated sharing my friend Simon Kaplan's story with you. He is a genuine one percenter, and a legacy worth learning from. Now here comes a chapter with an update on the Life Chest. We've been leading up to this chapter from the very first *Pumptitude* book. I hope by now you have a Life Chest, and you've been building your own legacy.

# One Percenter: Gino Wickman, Founder, EOS Worldwide

An author and business developer like no other, Gino Wickman gets it. His books, *Traction* and *Get a Grip*, are essential business reading for any successful executive trying to drive discipline, process, and ultimate achievement in their plan. With all his success, he remains humble and genuine in helping companies and people like me to achieve their best. Gino is a true one percenter.

|||||||||||||||||||||||||||||||||||||||||||||||||||||||||||||||||||||||||||||||||||||||||||||||||||||||||

Gino Wickman is the creator of EOS (the Entrepreneurial Operating System®), a practical method for helping companies achieve greatness. His system and tools have helped over 10,000 companies. He is also the founder of EOS Worldwide, an organization with an international team of EOS Implementers who work hands-on with leadership teams of companies, helping them implement EOS. Gino is also the author of two books, the award-winning best seller *Traction* and *Get a Grip*, which have sold tens of thousands of copies.

|||||||||||||||||||||||||||||||||||||||||||||||||||||||||||||||||||||||||||||||||||||||||||||||||||||||||

When Kim asked me to contribute to this chapter on leadership, it was flattering and I was thrilled to help. He asked me to share how I stay driven, focused, motivated and inspired. This is my formula:

It's simple. Our organization and I have a clear ten-year target, a three-year picture, and a one-year plan. In addition, we set a handful of quarterly priorities that we stay laser-focused on, which then direct our daily activities. Every night before I go to bed, I plan the next day so that my subconscious is working on the next day while I sleep. I wake up ready to take on the next day.

As a result of the above, we don't get distracted by "shiny stuff," which are any distractions that are not in alignment with our vision and goals.

In addition, we look to this vision, as well as five core values (be humbly confident, grow or die, help first, do the right thing, and do what you say) to make every decision, and we surround ourselves with people who are in alignment with the same vision and values.

In addition, we absolutely obsess about providing value to our clients through a constant understanding of their strengths, weaknesses, opportunities and threats. With this knowledge, we then provide the leadership, tools and direction to get everything they want from their lives and businesses.

As trite as they may seem, I also live by four basic rules taught to me by my mentor Dan Sullivan in every situation:

1. Show up on time
2. Do what you say
3. Finish what you start
4. Say "please" and "thank you"

# — Chapter 11 —

# LIFE CHEST

*If one person remembers you,*
*you live on.—Kim Yost*

Throughout the *Pumptitude* series, we've been describing the Life Chest project and the importance that it has had on my life and many others. To get the real story, however, you have to read my wife Donna's book. She describes in much greater detail the adventures she's had as the CEO of Life2000 and her quest to sell a million Life Chests in the years to come. By the time you read this book, Life Chests will have hit three channels for sales—furniture stores, funeral homes, and online sales at www.thelifechest.com. Hundreds of people are already enjoying the value of their own Life Chest. So if you haven't already, have a look at www.thelifechest.com to learn more. But first, enjoy this chapter.

## 55) Life Chest, revised—Donna's trip to China

Just over one year ago, I was at the High Point Furniture Show, a show I have attended for almost 30 years. The show is intense in terms of the number of exhibits I try to get to and the meetings that are scheduled around a large collection of buildings spread throughout the High Point area. Several hours a day are spent running here and there, trying to accomplish as much as I can in five days. There are dinners, awards nights and keynote speakers that are also vying for my time so covering all exhibit halls is almost impossible. There are hundreds, maybe thousands of products to see.

After spending several days at the show, I received a call from Tony Dragich, someone I mentored in the past, who was out and about searching through all of the remarkable wares at the show. "Kim, I'm in the accessory building and I am looking at a Life Chest! It looks a lot like the Life Chests you made, only it isn't yours! Don't you have a trademark? I think these guys are copying you. They are calling it something else but the concept is the same. I think you should investigate—your trademark is being infringed upon!"

Well, sure enough, I took a walk over to where Tony had seen the "counterfeit chests," and there they were, the same size, the same promotional idea, even made by the very factory that had manufactured my Original Life Chests. I immediately dialed my wife Donna and, well, the rest is history.

What I am about to share with you is a story I can hardly believe myself. It's what happens when you truly believe in something and you have a deep passion for making your dreams come true.

You see, right from day one when I met Donna, I had been sharing stories about the Life Chest project, how I started it and where I wanted the project to go. Of course, with the career that I have and the passion I have for that career and writing these books, the Life Chest project was lying dormant by choice so I could focus on my current purpose, Art Van Furniture. But when it appeared there had been some resurrection going on by what I would have to call a competitor or would-be counterfeiter, I had to take action. I immediately called Donna and reported the infringement and waited to see what she would say.

As I predicted, she jumped to the challenge. When I suggested she might have to get on a plane to protect the trademark and see what was going on, there was no hesitation. She was immediately engaged in protecting my dream from being taken by these tricksters. Within two short weeks, Chinese travel visa in hand, Donna was off to China, by herself, to battle it out with the people who were taking my idea and running with it. Well, what has occurred from there is nothing short of a miracle and here is that story.

Donna jumped on a plane for the 14-hour flight to Shanghai. I had arranged to have a colleague of mine meet her the morning after her arrival to spend a few days getting a bit of advice for the travel and experiences on which she was about to embark. Catherine had moved to Shanghai to work at a company I had started in Shanghai to help The Brick with the processes involved in procuring merchandise from the Chinese markets. Catherine spearheaded the project and had been living in Shanghai for eight years as leader of this company, First Oceans.

Catherine met Donna at her hotel and toured her through the streets of Shanghai for three days. The two had wonderful adventures, from walking the street markets to dining in the French Quarter of Old Shanghai. They shopped, ate, went to a concert, and walked through amazing art galleries. All the while, Catherine shared the dos and don'ts of traveling through China. After the three days of quick learning, Catherine bid Donna a fond farewell with wishes of safe travel, hoping her instructions had been adequately absorbed to keep Donna on track and fruitful in her endeavors.

After some misadventures at the Shanghai airport (you'll have to read Donna's book for all the details), Donna flew to southern China. Thankfully, my good friend Colin had made arrangements to have a driver pick her up at the airport and take her to her hotel. She got there without any difficulties; although, she shared the highway with several transport trucks tightly crammed with animals headed for a fate that none of us would like to imagine. Staring eyeball-to-eyeball with several of them affected her appetite for days and still has her thinking about becoming a vegetarian.

Bright and early the next morning, Donna had her driver take her to the factory to meet with the people who were marketing my idea under their new label. At the gate to the factory, Donna introduced herself and mentioned that she had an appointment. Reluctantly, the gatekeeper walked over to his gatehouse, picked up a phone and began a conversation that dragged on for what seemed to be an hour. When he finally came back to address my wife, he said, "No meetings today." Donna tried again, "Sir, I have a meeting this morning, please check again. I came all the way to your factory from the United States, and I must see your owner now." The guard just stood there. Donna didn't really know what to do next, so she stood there also. She smiled at the guard and said, "Well, I guess I will have to wait here until the person I was supposed to meet comes through the gate and then I will see them that way." They stood that way for some time, saying nothing, just standing there. After quite some time, the guard seemed to get a little irritated and got back on the phone. Sure enough, the gate opened and he gestured for her to go on in.

Donna's internal pumptitude is what got her through these gates.

174

Once in the factory, Donna was ushered into a meeting room. She sat there for over half an hour until the door opened and a young lady named Theresa entered the room. Apologizing, she said that those whom Donna had come to see were not in that day. She offered a tour of the factory, so Donna went through the whole facility with her Asian tour guide. Sure enough, the product line was being made virtually the same way as my Original Life Chest. Even the packaging was the same, with the same photo design on the outside of the boxes. Donna reminded the tour guide of the trademark that existed on the product they were producing, sharing that we were onto the fact that they were using my idea. They agreed that yes, they were copying, and then asked if they could have us as partners. Well, I guess everything happens for a reason because once Donna returned from that trip and told me everything she learned, the Original Life Chest project was revived!

Not only did Donna investigate the infringement, she came back saying, "You know, one way to get these people to stop what they are doing is to revive the project and do a much better job. I can up the ante and when they see what Life2000 can do, they will no longer have the courage to compete."

Not only has my wife developed, designed, and put into production a whole new collection of Life Chests, she has brought my daughter Ashley into the whirlwind.

Within two months, Donna had hired a full on design team, went down to North Carolina on two separate occasions to develop a number of designs and was on her way back across the world to find her factories. While away, she dissolved the relationship with the factory that had previously manufactured the initial designs for Life2000 and tapped into some of my contacts and friends to find a factory that could produce higher quality product at more competitive prices than the old factory.

She also visited several countries to prospect in case there would ever be need for other sources. As development continued, Donna wanted access to a premium factory to develop an heirloom-quality line of Life Chests that would be truly worthy of the people's lives they were to represent. Within weeks she had met and engaged one of the premier manufacturers in the U.S. to design and manufacture this premium line of Life Chests.

She also pursued a connection close to home so there could be a "Made in USA" product line if needed. After several visits and months of creativity, these Life Chests are about to arrive in her warehouse. Yes, Donna has a warehouse, along with an office where she and her small team attack the world, vowing that they are going to create a movement of people who are committed to leaving a legacy in no time.

The Life Chest project is further evidence of the power of the *Pumptitude* principles. They are not theoretical or hypothetical; they are tried and tested by real life.

## 56) If one person remembers you, you live on

Since Donna's return from China and bringing my daughter Ashley into the Life2000 company, the two of them have been traveling to shows, showing our 32 sample chests, and sharing our story with anyone who will listen. They are working with The Pink Fund, a Detroit-area charity that operates on a national level providing financial help for women who are undergoing treatment for breast cancer. The Pink Fund helps pay bills for these struggling women, helping to give them some room to focus on getting better. They are also working with the All Veteran Parachute Team and their Therapy in the Air program for soldiers wounded on active duty.

These girls have found their place in the world through the Life Chest project. The reaction from everyone the Life Chest story touches is so overwhelmingly positive, it is as though there is a divine intervention going on. Faith in this project has always been there, but when you mix faith and passion together… well, you just have to see Donna and Ashley's faces when they talk about what they have seen and what they are doing. It has been overwhelming to hear firsthand from people what having a Life Chest brings to them in terms of the simple peace of knowing they will be remembered and their legacy will be preserved as they wish it to be.

Ashley Yost and Donna Yost, Troy Michigan office for Life 2000 Limited

Donna is committed to creating many opportunities, from getting veterans back to work and developing a line of Life Chests that are American-made right here in Michigan to providing breast cancer survivors with ways to keep their legacies alive.

## 57) Life partners, business partners, family partners

The Life Chest project also gives me an opportunity to talk about Donna and me being partners together in life and in business. Being a life partner can enhance a business relationship and being a business partner can enhance a life relationship. This is the ultimate magical balance where both spouses are aligned on every aspect of their lives. The lesson here is to ensure that your spouse is tuned into every aspect of your life so that there can be maximum sharing and openness. Donna and I are engaged in a work of love, art, business and life. It has been an adventure.

When spouses work together as one, they can achieve anything. Donna and I run forward together, one doesn't have to drag the other. We are bigger together than we could ever have been separately.

## 58) Say "Yes" to the Chest

For the Life Chest project, my daughter Ashley Yost is using her degree in radio and television to produce videos and sharing the remarkable stories she and Donna are uncovering as they travel and talk to all of the amazing people they are meeting along the way. I have never seen my daughter so engaged and excited about her career. She tells me she is dreaming about all the things she wants to do to get these people's Life Chest stories out into the world. Here are some notes from Ashley about her experience with the project.

*Say yes to the chest—I did!*

*You might think that being the daughter of two extraordinary people is a tall order to fill growing up, that the bars would be set so high you would never be able to reach them. In my case, I have been lucky enough to have had the support of both parents, guiding me and supporting me in any endeavor, big or small.*

*Not a day goes by where I am not thankful to have these two people in my life. To be able to call them my parents is a blessing. I aspire to learn from them daily and although my rebellious and stubborn side may come out sometimes, they are always there being patient and helping to guide me back on track toward the right path to success.*

Attitude determines Altitude

Ashley says Yes to the Chest

*The Life Chest has been a part of my life since I was a baby. I always knew of this concept but never expected it would flourish into this amazing business opportunity and team that I am now part of.*

*My father always taught me the importance of working as a team. When I used to play soccer as a little girl, there were times when I couldn't play or didn't feel like playing and my dad would make me sit on the side lines to cheer on my team. Maybe this theory worked, as my soccer team started out being the least likely to succeed and by the end of the season we had won the championship!*

*Throughout my life, my father would talk about how he loved his job. I have learned that being passionate, positive and prepared makes for a great recipe to achieve your goals, not only in your career but in your overall success in everything you do.*

*My father gave me a book called One Word That Will Change Your Life by Jon Gordon (see Chapter 1, #2). I thoroughly enjoyed it, and applied the concept by choosing one word for the year to keep me on track and make me a star—not only in work but also in my life. My father's word is relentless, and though that is a word I would never choose for myself, it fits my father to a T. He attacks situations, he never gives up, and he is relentless in every aspect of his life—both career and personal.*

*My word is shine! I want to shine in my tasks at work, I want to shine in my relationships, and I want to shine so bright this year that I make an impact on everything and anything that I set my mind to.*

*While many advise against working for and with family members, I was excited and very interested in getting an inside view of what makes Kim and Donna Yost tick and how they got to be where they are. I was willing to work hard, but I did not expect to love my job. Now I can say that is exactly what has happened. I love my job!*

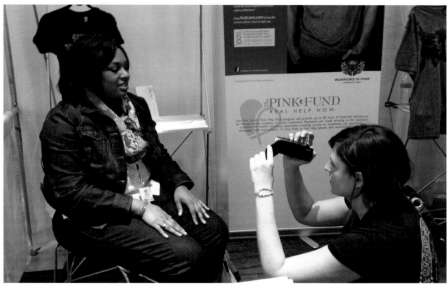

Ashley Yost filming at C4YW (Cancer for Young Women) in Seattle

As you have read, the Life Chest project is a great one. Ashley's education, talent and passion are really making a difference.

## 59) The Yost factor—what box?

In addition to Ashley, Donna has another driven, high achieving team member. As you read her story, you will soon see why; between Donna, Ashley and Julie, this project is destined for success.

Julie Kay Donegan is Donna's executive assistant, and she handles operations for the Life Chest project. She offered these observations about her time with us:

Julie Donegan working "outside the box"

*The phrase "think outside the box" seems a bit overused. After all, who decides where the borders of the box lie? Has thinking outside the box become predictable and cliché? Regardless, I don't have to worry about any hypothetical objects. At Life2000 Ltd. the Yosts have created an environment free of any allegorical boxes and have instead taught me three very meaningful things about building a company and an internal entrepreneurial spirit:*

*1. Be a "Yes!" person*

*2. Don't dwell on obstacles*

*3. Share ideas and future goals*

*I quickly learned to embrace "Yes!" from the very beginning. At the end of an interview at The Townhouse*

Bistro in Birmingham, Donna Yost asked me if I would join her for a product development trip in two days as a continuation of our interview. Instantly, the obstacles popped in my head: "Who will cover my shift at work? Won't flights be outrageously expensive?" But I knew in my gut that this opportunity should not be passed up. So I said "Yes!" and everything naturally slid into place. Since then it has been an exciting journey and partnership for the two of us.

Life2000 Ltd. is a place that opens minds and fosters ideas. Mr. Yost taught me the significance of mind mapping in our very first meeting. Mind maps are the illustrated flow of ideas—brainstorming at its most rudimentary level. Before joining the Life2000 team, I used outlines as my preferred method for organizing ideas: linear, clean, and methodical—perfect for me as I worked in research and prepared for midterms. The major fault with outlines, however, lies within their primary benefit; with all the structure, there is little to no room for expansion or change in direction. Roman numerals stand like obedient chess pieces, revealing only the thought process of the creator. No other ideas or perspectives are invited. Outlines certainly qualify as inside the box.

Mind mapping, on the other hand, creates more room for building off original ideas, editing, and allowing others to be a part of the conversation. It is an organic and creative process, and it certainly does not fit into any box. Such a simple idea has been a major influence on my professional growth while working on The Life Chest.

Mentorship through the invitation of ideas—not the dictation of them—sets the Yosts apart. This is what I call "The Yost Factor." In no other business environment would an entry-level employee be granted the frequent opportunity to sit down with a CEO, gain knowledge, *and openly share ideas. It is an opportunity for which I am grateful, and I acknowledge its significant impact on my professional growth and development. I look forward to continued lifelong learning, mind mapping, and personal growth through the invaluable lessons of Kim and Donna Yost.*

Julie Donegan, Kim Yost and Donna Yost

As we leave this chapter, I'm reminded about the fact that the Life Chest is so much more than capturing your past, present and future life. In reading Ashley and Julie's stories, it's easy to see that it's having a benefit well beyond one I could imagine. What an absolute blessing that the Life Chest came into my life over 30 years ago.

Linda and I will soon be embarking on one of our biggest challenges to date as a writing team. Our fourth book will be all about the Life Chest. It will tell the story of its conception, which occurred during the building of the Great Wall of China. It continues three centuries into the future to the story of Bernie and Josh in Appendix A in *Maximum Pumptitude*. This fourth book, entitled *The Adventures Within the Life Chest*, will have more stories, drama, sex and violence than any other story told in history. Stay tuned; we'll keep you posted. For now, get ready for the final chapter of *Internal Pumptitude* about the ultimate reward for all of us one percenters.

## One Percenter: Jack Krasula, President, Trustinus, LLC

One of the highlights in my Life Chest is a recording of a show called *Anything's Possible*, hosted by Jack Krasula (see Chapter 4, #17). I was asked to share my life story during Jack's show, and he was kind enough to record and document the story. I've also had the pleasure of being in Jack's home and viewing his collection of sports memorabilia—clearly the biggest in the world. Spending time with Jack and listening to his stories is a joy and an inspiration in itself. He has interviewed hundreds of one percenters and high achievers on Sunday nights at nine o'clock on his radio show. There is no one I've ever met with more of an appreciation for building a legacy, learning from that, and applying it to the future.

Trustinus, LLC President Jack Krasula is formerly the founder, CEO, and president of Decision Consultants, Inc. (DCI), the largest privately-held professional information technology services firm in the U.S. Krasula sold DCI to Ciber, Inc. in May 2002.

Jack started his company in 1976 and grew the company from a one-person operation to a 1,800-plus employee firm with $160 million in revenue. Unlike other companies with empty mission statements, Jack did everything he could to ensure his philosophy was remembered—and lived. Today, Jack is carrying on his philosophy and approach to people with Trustinus, LLC, a world-class provider of executive search services, and Star Tickets, a full-service ticketing provider.

Jack is also the radio show host of *Anything is Possible* on NewsTalk 760 WJR, a weekly inspirational show on Sunday evenings highlighting successful people who rose from humble beginnings.

Jack received an undergraduate degree from Lewis University and then went on to obtain an MBA from Loyola University.

||||||||||||||||||||||||||||||||||||||||||||||||||||||||||||||||||||||||||||||||||||||||||||||||||||||

In 1976, when Krasula was only 26 years old, he launched his own company, Decision Consultants, Inc., a temp service that trains and places computer programmers. DCI started slowly, but it caught the boom of the 1980s and now has 1,800 full-time employees, offices in 12 cities and annual revenues of $160 million. It is the largest privately-held company in its field. In the hallway of DCI's headquarters in suburban Detroit, Krasula has posted a personal letter from Zig Ziglar, the evangelical sales guru. "You can have everything in life you want," Ziglar wrote, "if you will just help enough other people get what they want."

What Krasula thinks his employees want, above all, is appreciation. So twice a month, he spends four hours writing a personal thank you note on every employees' paycheck.

Krasula's office feels less like a corporate nerve center than a rec room. He has a dozen baseball caps on his bookshelf, a train engine made of clarinet parts on the coffee table, and a framed doodle of Mickey Mouse drawn by Walt Disney himself on the wall. On another wall, he has a crucifix, a letter from Norman Vincent Peale, and a framed motivational speech by Vince Lombardi.

"Everything in his office is ultimately about success," says Lee Tonnies, one of Krasula's key lieutenants for 18 years. "That is the core of Jack. He likes to talk about why people are successful and compliments those who are."

# — Chapter 12 —

# THE ULTIMATE REWARD

*You can't change the future if you're*
*focusing on the past.*
*—Source unknown.*

If you can continue to work hard, you can get to this point of the ultimate reward. I am doing more now than I've ever done. I feel like my capacity is expanding daily because I am so engaged in what I'm doing. Growing older can positively correlate with increased activity rather than the other way round. With the right focus and conditioning, our energy can be directed in a way that yields phenomenal results.

This is a great shout out to those people in their 50s and 60s— we can become better as we grow older! We're only as old as how we feel about life. It's all about doing less of the things that don't matter and more of the things that do.

## 60) No regrets

As you start to read our final chapter, it is important for us to put to bed this incredible and powerful human behavior: having and constantly thinking about our regrets. Throughout the *Pumptitude* series, we have encouraged you to look forward and have a clear vision of where you want to go. Regrets are a paralyzing emotion. They give you huge anxiety and douse your excitement about the future. If you focus on your regrets, in most cases it will eliminate your enthusiasm about the future. Diane Wells, assistant to Chairman Art Van, recently sent me a great quote from a poem by Mary Engelbreit. It sums up the idea of having no regrets.

*Don't look back, you're not going that way.*

We are all prone to wanting to revise the past and change decisions, actions, and in some cases, our own history. Guess what? You can't. Get over it. Live in the moment, and the moments to come. People who are constantly regretting everything are usually negative, depressed and downright boring. We must avoid these people at all costs and definitely avoid becoming these people! Whenever I'm tempted to regret something, I think of a quote I heard several years ago, "We should not look to the past for regrets, but for knowledge we can apply to the future."

## 61) Perseverance and adversity

*Perseverance: to persist in a state, enterprise, or undertaking in spite of counterinfluences, opposition, or discouragement.*
*—Merriam-Webster Dictionary*

Sometimes the adversity that stops people from getting things done is simply that person's own mind being off track. We all experience a multitude of deterrents on the path to our dreams and commitments, unless we can figure out how to persevere through these distractions.

I believe the best way to persevere through challenges is to keep the goal in mind, focus on readying yourself for each step of the way, and plan for how you will battle through when these deterrents crop up.

Everyone has days where the outer world affects our inner world. If our I-Pump has become a strong habit, this will overrule these distractions. Tap into your optimistic commitment to winning even if it is just winning over distractions. Imagine how much more productive you will be when you persevere!

Perseverance trumps adversity every time.

## 62) Life's biggest challenge

*The biggest challenge in life is being satisfied with what you have while in pursuit of what you want.—Jim Rohn*

This section was contributed by Kevin Gilfillan, and I know you will enjoy it.

*Do you know anyone who seems very unhappy with their life even though they have a good family, a good job, a nice home, plenty of food to eat, etc.? They just don't seem to see the good in their life.*

*It's not uncommon; it's probably more common than we think. People sometimes tend to see only the things they don't have or the stuff they'd like to have and miss out on so much of the good they do have.*

*Jim Rohn's simple statement is a good reminder that we should start each day with a sense of gratitude, by counting our blessings. As we appreciate our advantages, we will begin to enjoy our days and understand the mystery and wonder of our lives, thereby setting us up for greater success and more reward.*

*If you aren't happy with what you currently have and then you get more, you'll only be more unhappy. More only brings more of what we already are. And so we need to be happy with what we have so we can be happy with what we will get.*

*Pursuing what we want is also good. Wanting more out of life, wanting to grow more, become more, and have more is an important part of building a successful life. Set goals, have a vision of who you want to become, and what you want to have. Enjoy the challenge. Just don't let your desires blind you to the blessings in your life.*

## 63) Save the parade—giving back makes for good business and good karma

Throughout my life, I have realized the importance of giving back and sharing. I've been very fortunate to have been mentored by individuals who have not only taught me this, but have illustrated it in every part of their lives. For example, both Mr. Bill Comrie and Mr. Art Van Elslander have given back countless dollars to their communities and employees. I'm going to share with you four stories that are about giving back. You'll hear about the positive effects on the people who have received, and, unquestionably, on the people who gave.

First, as CEO and President of The Brick stores, I personally experienced a level of giving back to employees that was like no other. When Mr. Bill Comrie sold The Brick company several years ago, he gave back over $45 million out of the selling proceeds to hundreds of Brick employees. The money was divided using an equation that we worked on and was based on length of service and position within the company.

When Bill made the decision to give millions of dollars back to his employees, he did it for three reasons: (1) It was these employees, over the years, who had built such a terrific company that investors now wanted to purchase from him. (2) He had a deep feeling of responsibility to better the lives of the people that he had spent so many years with building The Brick. He knew that these monies would go to help his employees for their future. (3) He knew that so many other companies were sold in Canada for, in some cases, a lot more than The Brick, and the owners gave nothing back to their employees. This type of selfishness was not in Bill's DNA.

We later received amazing letters from countless employees about what Bill's money had done to change their lives and secure their futures. Many of them now had the ability to send their children to college and university. Many of them now had the ability to pay off their mortgages. Many of them now had the ability to buy well overdue new cars. The list went on.

My next story is one I learned from Jim Rohn. He uses the example of a shoeshine. Let's say you get a shoeshine at a street-side stand or an airport booth, and you tip the young man or woman with half of what you believed the tip was worth. For the rest of the day, when you look at your shiny shoes or get compliments about how shiny they are, you will remember that they came from you half-tipping the person who shined them.

Let's say instead that you give a few extra dollars as a well-deserved tip. Now for the entire day, when you look down at your shiny shoes, or when people remark about how amazing they look, you can enjoy the good feeling that came from being generous and giving back. You will remember that the shoe shiner added value to your day, and in turn, you added value to theirs.

In my case, for years I have traveled the world and over-tipped for shoeshines, and I also over-tipped waiters, cab drivers, hotel bellmen, and several others. Believe me when I say to you that I have not only received and benefitted from the joy of doing so, I have come to realize that by giving back and sharing your success, you benefit in so many ways you can't even measure.

My third story is one I heard months ago. There is a business executive living in Los Angeles, California, who gives back in a way I never could have imagined. We have to assume that he is a very successful businessman because for years he has been giving $100,000 a year in cash, anonymously, to hundreds of needy families. His method of giving back these thousands of dollars is very unusual. He shows up with no fanfare, unannounced, and dressed very casually in food banks, shelters, homeless hostels, hospitals, and many other locations where people are in great need. He carries white, unmarked envelopes, each containing hundreds of dollars, and when he comes across an individual or family in need, he simply hands over this white envelope and says, "I hope this benefits you," and then quietly moves on.

You could say he's like a modern-day Zorro or Lone Ranger, but in his case, he doesn't wear a mask. The simplicity of his giving, and the timeliness of it, overshadows his need to wear one. Now no one knows who this business executive is, but you can be guaranteed of two things: (1) he has changed the lives of many, and (2) he himself has been changed positively because of the act.

My final story of the power of giving back is from several years ago when Mr. Van had an opportunity to save the annual Thanksgiving Day parade in Detroit, now known as America's Thanksgiving Parade®. This iconic parade was in financial

America's Thanksgiving Parade®., Detroit

jeopardy, as several sponsors had decided to discontinue their support. Mr. Van learned that the parade needed almost a quarter of a million dollars, or it could no longer continue to exist. This is a big figure even today, but in the early 1990s, this was really a large sum of money. It was a difficult decision, but Mr. Van decided to save the parade.

Over the last 25 years, the parade has continued to grow and thrive because of Mr. Van's generosity, continued contributions, and involvement. Today, Mr. Van is cited as the single individual who saved the parade. Millions of children and families have enjoyed this parade year after year. The benefits to him, his family, and the entire Art Van organization have been priceless. No one could have ever imagined that an act of generosity some 25 years ago would have touched the hearts and minds of so many people today.

When all of us get to Stage 6 of life (*Maximum Pumptitude*, Chapter 11, #68), from age 58 and beyond, or when we are in a position of financial security at any age, remember to give back and share. You can be guaranteed that your success in life will be a direct reflection of your level of generosity.

Detroit Jazz Festival Float

## 64) Winning is everything

In *Pumptitude* (Chapter 5, 32, "Play to Win"), I quoted Brian Tracy as saying, "Winning isn't everything, but wanting to is." With all respect to Brian, I now say, **winning *is* everything; losing is not so much fun.**

In completing this book and reading through all the contributions from our high achievers, top performers and true one percenters, I've come to realize that winning is reserved for a small percentage. Many are just not prepared to put in the effort, do the hard work, make the sacrifices, take the risks, apply the persistence, reinvent themselves, or practice the many other behaviors that you have been reading about.

The Winners' Circle is not for everybody, but those who arrive there get to enjoy life with the volume at 10. The good news is that there's plenty of room for you because so few people will do the work to get here.

Wanting to be in the Winners' Circle without putting in any effort reminds me of a line I've heard, "Everybody wants to go to heaven, but nobody is willing to die to get there."

Don't forget that there is another reason why winning feels so great. Positive mental endorphins are released directly into the brain when people feel the extreme excitement of achieving goals, winning at competition, or doing something darn amazing. So continue to feed your brain with positive mental endorphins and enjoy living in the end zone. It's a great place to be.

## 65) Step out of your comfort zone

A big part of what I do is coaching, challenging and downright irritating people to become more than they sometimes see in themselves. We just recently completed the first round of an eight-week course, titled "The One Percenter Course" at Art Van. It was targeted for sales managers, essentially the seconds-in-command who want to become managers in stores doing around $20 million of sales with approximately 100 employees.

My wife Donna showing she is a one percenter, sky diving with Mike Elliott, founder of allveteranparachuteteam.com, Fort Bragg, North Carolina

The course was on Mondays nights from 6:00–8:00 p.m. Several of our vice presidents presented each Monday on a variety of topics, which were all focused on getting these sales managers ready for their own stores and their own teams. We explained at the start that their final assignment would be to prepare, submit, and then present a business plan. Their goal was to incorporate the topics from the weekly classes into their own plan that would drive, improve or change something about our company.

In the first few weeks, you could see that there was high eagerness and excitement to learn, but we also saw that for some students, this course took them too far out of their comfort zone. Fear got the better of them, and they dropped the course. We had challenged them to go to a place that they had never been before. We challenged them to develop a business plan and present that business plan to an audience of vice presidents and fellow students upon completion of the course.

As the weeks progressed, we could see how the remaining students were growing from the knowledge they were getting. In fact, two of the sales managers became store managers and got their stores at the halfway mark! By the end of the course, we had received many excellent business plans that were well thought out and included financials, a compelling story, and an execution plan.

During the final night of the class, Mr. Art Van Elslander, our chairman, Mr. Gary Van Elslander, our president, and several vice presidents were on hand to give out awards to various students. In their acceptance speeches, the sales managers indicated that they were challenged, stressed, had lost sleep, had pushed beyond the knowledge that they had, and had grown like never before. They expressed incredible appreciation for the opportunity to participate. So what these one percenter students can teach all of us is that it is good to have a life of learning; it is good to be challenged out of our comfort zones; it is good to put away our fears of failure in exchange for the opportunity of success. As I watched the graduation ceremony, it was overwhelming and gratifying to see some of the ideas in the *Pumptitude* books come to life.

A special shout out to Mr. Casey Wooley for **Best Business Plan Overall** and to Lindsay Loprest and Wayne Hollars for second and third place. Finally, the **Most Creative Business Plan** was awarded to Cheryl Cruttenden.

## 66) Be a mummy or a purple cow

What I'm about to tell you may seem odd and darn right weird, but it's meant to illustrate that when it comes to building your legacy, you cannot predict how your actions may impact generations to come.

This story takes us back to when I was approximately 23 years old, and a buyer for Woodward's department store in Vancouver, British Columbia. Woodward's had buying offices throughout Europe and Asia, and we would travel for weeks at a time sourcing products. In some cases, we sourced products for special promotions that would highlight specific countries.

I was traveling outside of Bombay, India, visiting several hand-woven area rug factories, and it was on this trip where a great legacy was uncovered. One particular factory had amazing carpets that I was in the process of purchasing and shipping in a 40-foot container for an India promotion. In my usual stone-turning fashion when visiting factories, I was going through the back rooms, scouring through all the nooks and crannies, looking for odd and different things.

I came across an approximately 300-year-old mummy in the most amazing condition. I negotiated with the factory owner to include the mummy with the order so I could feature it in my display with all my rugs from India. He was initially reluctant to give up this family heirloom, but he eventually decided that the order I was giving him was far more important than holding on to one of his ancestors.

Fast forward three months, and boy did that mummy ever have a strong odor when we took it out of that shipping container! I displayed it in all its glory in amongst my rugs during the India promotion. On the evening of its preview, our chairman, several board members, and the Indian consulate came to visit my display. It was then I found out that no matter how old a dead body may be, you cannot remove it from a country without meeting strict regulations and completing the proper paperwork. We got into quite a skirmish with the Indian consulate and had to send the mummy back.

Nothing I have ever bought, overseas or domestic, created more excitement, more conversation, or more visits than my 300-year-old mummy. It was the buzz for months. Imagine this mummy, traveling all the way from India, hundreds of years after his death, to Vancouver, British Columbia, to be put on display during a department store's show featuring products from India. What a legacy!

The other learning here is that all of us should have such excitement in each of our lives. Whether we're living or dead, thousands of people should want to come see us because of our uniqueness and because of who we are. This mummy was just that—very unique. This story also ties in with the theme of a book I've been handing out to my colleagues and business associates, called *The Purple Cow* by Seth Godin.

Godin describes his travels across the French countryside, where he saw hundreds of beautiful brown cows. As they kept driving past all these brown cows, they stopped even noticing them. It occurred to him how exciting it would be to spot, let's say, a purple cow, in and amongst all those brown ones. The premise of his book, and the moral of my story, is that if you want to stand out with anything you do, you need to either be a 300-year-old mummy or a purple cow.

As you go about your life, as we've been describing throughout the *Pumptitude* series, we want you to be bold, be unique, make a difference, be remembered, and create a legacy. To this day, several people I worked with all those years ago still refer to the "Yost mummy," and use it as a term for doing something out of the ordinary. May your life be filled with mummies!

## 67) Why we do what we do

In Chapter 8, I referenced Simon Sinek and his amazing book, *Start With Why*. He explains that while most of us start by talking about what we do, then how we do it, and finally we might look at why, the Golden Circle approach is to **start with the why**. Individuals who do this, especially leaders, are far more inspiring.

I took this to heart and composed this WHY statement for the Art Van leadership team:

> *Everything we do will challenge the status quo. We will go to places we have never been before. As a result, we will never want to go back. Our vision and mission is to clearly differentiate ourselves from others, along with having the need to constantly and never-endingly improve. We strive to be smart, hungry and humble, and live with purpose, drive and style. We promote and inspire others, and we live to make a difference.*

At Art Van, we are creating a context that enables people to perform at their absolute best—the most fertile environment for anyone to be the best that they can be, a place where winners come to win.

All we can do is create the environment and set an example. Individuals within this context have to seize the opportunity and make the most of it. Art Van associates have to live the WHY in order to thrive, and we invite them to do this every day, by establishing standards the people have to meet and exceed.

The Art Van WHY statement debuted on June 13, 2013, at a black-tie dinner at the Grand Hyatt hotel in New York City during which I was presented with an American Heritage Award from the Anti-Defamation League. The event raised $750,000 for the ADL.

I was introduced by Larry Rogers, CEO of Sealy North America and the other recipient of the American Heritage Award. He reviewed everything that I have achieved over my career. My daughter Ashley attended the event with us, and she shared that hearing this summary was an amazing opportunity to understand what I have accomplished.

I tell you, this is what every father dreams of—making his children proud and helping them understand what his life has been about. It was extraordinary to be able to celebrate an evening like this with my two primary stakeholders—my spouse and my daughter. My wife Donna is my present and my daughter Ashley is my future.

Hearing Ashley's reaction was a powerful reminder that as I strive to be a role model for all the leaders at Art Van, I, and we all, need to be a role model for both our families and our colleagues.

## 68) Building your legacy

*We get one opportunity in life, one chance at life to do whatever you're going to do, and lay your foundation and make whatever mark you're going to make. Whatever legacy you're going to leave; leave your legacy!—Ray Lewis*

Legacy. From as far back as I can remember, this word has not only intrigued me, it has taunted, tempted and maybe even tortured me. I could see how important it truly is to preserve the foundation each and every life has bestowed upon us so future generations can understand and build on what it is we spend our lifetimes cultivating and learning. I have poured my soul into creating a movement to encourage everyone to commit to that purpose.

Leaving a legacy that is worthy of generations to come is no small task. A legacy is something you leave behind, expecting nothing in return; it isn't for you, it is for future. It is what engages families in the present by planning for the future and remembering the past. It is the pure essence of someone's soul that can be felt by jogging the memory through photos, or books, or ticket stubs, or maybe even just by the smell of something that the person wore.

When I was much younger, I felt invincible. I guess to some degree we all do, that is until you find out about mortality and that nothing is forever. Or can it? When I lost my friend Scony in my teenage years (I wrote about Scony in Chapter 9, #47), it was my first scuff with death and the first time my young mind had to wrestle with the fact that we are fragile. Thoughts of Scony have continued to pop up throughout my life, bringing him back into my life one way or another many times. But as we age and our memories fade, how do we preserve those precious moments from disappearing forever?

As you know from reading my previous books and Chapter 11 of this book, I preserve my memories and my legacy in Life Chests—and I have many of them. I have a Life Chest for my life's work, housing many achievements in my career, all the way back to when I was 19 years old. I have another Life Chest that keeps personal trinkets and tales of a young man's life, including tall tales of catching massive fish with my adopted father and his pals, as well as the birth of my daughter and stepping stones in her life.

What I witness every single day when Donna pops out of bed, or when she is sneakily communicating with her factories and designers at all hours of the night from under the covers so she won't wake me up, is true I-Pump. What she and her team have accomplished in under a year is nothing short of remarkable, and what is so amazing is that her whole team is taking on this project with that same passion. You are only as good as the company you keep, and Donna is proof of that!

As you read in Chapter 11, my daughter Ashley is also working on the Life Chest project; when I see her come to work and hear her describe what she is learning and how excited she is, I can't imagine our lives without this dream of legacy.

Ashley has had her Life Chest from birth and when she goes through her chest or sneaks a peek in mine, it spawns conversation that would otherwise be forgotten. Every time she comes back from a conference and shares how many people she spoke to about what they would put in their Life Chest, it reminds me of why I love the project, why I worked so hard to start this movement, and why I am so proud to stand and watch Donna and her team take it to a new level.

Has this been easy? No. The many hours, the many miles traveled, and the many dollars spent threaten our commitment, but we do not buckle or let go of our dream and you cannot either. We must harness our internal pumptitude, our resilience and drive, and keep going.

This *Pumptitude* series is part of my legacy. Writing these books was my way of understanding my own thinking, almost becoming a public form of journaling. It's also my way of giving kudos to the great people and influences in my life. Writing is my discipline but also my passion and my joy. This is the power of the pen. Other one percenters are also using these books as their legacy because I have recognized their great achievements and asked them to tell their stories.

For one percenters in particular, leaving a legacy must be a priority, as you do the work that helps others see their path and better their lives. You must share your stories, save your mementoes and affect as many lives in a positive way as possible. The world needs leaders and when true leaders lead, they bring people with them and everyone wins.

So build your legacies, help create that movement that ensures all we share is passed on through generations to come. Have that legacy speak about who you are, what your essence is and who you want to be. Build your life so when generations from now open your Life Chest they will see that you put in your all, you didn't hold back and your legacy speaks for itself. Share your gifts with the world, and share your intimate tales with your loved ones and close friends. Shape the futures of those you want to influence. Most importantly, **live your legacy**!

## Art Van One Percenter: Gary Duncan, Vice President, Human Resources

It is so fitting to have Gary Duncan as our one percenter in our final chapter, "The Ultimate Reward." As a husband, father, grandfather, and successful executive, he is the epitome of that for which we all should strive. Anyone who knows Gary knows two things: one, he has a true desire to make you the best you can be; two, he's trying to break his family's perfect record of not being funny. As I've told Gary repeatedly, there hasn't been a funny Duncan for generations, and why he's trying to break a perfect record is beyond me. I'm pleased to introduce a great friend and colleague, Mr. Gary Duncan.

||||||||||||||||||||||||||||||||||||||||||||||||||||||||||||||||||||||||||||||||||||||||||||||||||

 A member of the Art Van Leadership Team since 2009, Gary is no stranger to retail. He has over 40 years of retail experience in the supermarket, mass merchandising, and consumer electronics fields. He has held positions in store operations, merchandising, buying, and human resources.

Over the last 25 years as a human resources professional, his experience has covered talent acquisition, training, organizational development, associate relations, labor relations, compensation, and benefits.

Reporting to the CEO, Gary oversees the entire human resources function at Art Van Furniture, a company of over 2,800 associates.

||||||||||||||||||||||||||||||||||||||||||||||||||||||||||||||||||||||||||||||||||||||||||||||||||

During my career I have been part of leadership teams that had to make difficult decisions, some leading to success and others to failure. Given the perspective of time, I see now that many of the decisions that lead to unsuccessful conclusions were motivated by a fear of failure. This fear led to decisions that attempted to minimize failure instead of maximizing success. Conversely, decisions motivated by an optimistic view of the future and a desire to do what is needed to succeed often lead to the success that was only visualized when the decision was made.

What I have learned from these experiences is that for success to be possible, an individual has to have confidence, both in themselves and in the team with which they are aligned, for no one can achieve success alone.

## INTERNAL PUMPTITUDE

I have always found my motivation to succeed to come from two directions, the first from within—an internal drive to achieve success and a personal desire for growth. The second source of my motivation has always come from those with whom I work. I have always felt most comfortable as a part of team of individuals whom I trust and respect. From trust and respect comes confidence, and from confidence comes the drive and effort that is necessary for success.

During my career I have been fortunate enough to find this kind of confidence and support twice—once with my first company and once with Art Van Furniture. Over the past four years, I have seen the leadership team at Art Van grow in many ways, but most noticeably in our confidence and sense of purpose. We stood up to the recession and succeeded in spite of the obstacles. We visualized our success and worked together to achieve that which we visualized.

As we embark in 2013 upon the most extensive growth in our company's history, we will need to call upon the confidence of every individual, as well as support one another in our efforts. It is a time for uncommon leadership and a total lack of fear.

# — Appendix A —

# INTERNAL PUMPTITUDE READING LIST

## Introduction

*Pumptitude*, by Kim Yost

*Maximum Pumptitude*, by Kim Yost with Donna Yost and Linda Dessau

## Chapter 1: The 68-Day Challenge

*Everything Counts*, by Gary Ryan Blair

*One Word that will Change Your Life*, by Dan Britton, Jimmy Page and Jon Gordon

## Chapter 3: One Percenters

*Success is a Choice*, by Rick Pitino and Bill Reynolds

*The Shark and the Goldfish*, by Jon Gordon

*Everyone Communicates, Few Connect*, by John C. Maxwell

*The Charge: Activating the 10 Human Drives That Make You Feel Alive*, by Brendon Burchard

*Talk to the Mirror*, by Florine Mark

## Chapter 4: No Fear

*The Miracle Morning*, by Hal Elrod

## Chapter 5: Habits That Can Change Your Life

*The 7 Habits of Highly Effective People*, by Stephen R. Covey

*The 8th Habit*, by Stephen R. Covey

*The Power of Habit*, by Charles Duhigg

## Chapter 7: Embrace Change

*Changeology*, by John C. Norcross,
Kristin Loberg, and Jonathon Norcross

## Chapter 8: Have Something to Fight For

*The Energy Bus*, by Jon Gordon and Ken Blanchard

*Start With Why*, by Simon Sinek

## Chapter 10: Uncommon Leadership

*Beyond Band of Brothers: The War Memoirs of Major Dick Winters*, by Major Dick Winters with Colonel Cole C. Kingseed

*Traction*, by Gino Wickman

*Get a Grip*, by Gino Wickman and Mike Paton

## Chapter 12: The Ultimate Reward

*The Purple Cow*, by Seth Godin

# — Appendix B —

# KIM'S TOP 100 BOOKS

1. *Lead Your Boss*, by John Baldoni

2. *Overpromise and Overdeliver*, by Rick Barrera

3. *The Future of Leadership*, by Warren Bennis, Gretchen M. Spreitzer and Thomas G. Cummings

4. *Everything Counts*, by Gary Ryan Blair

5. *Raving Fans*, by Ken Blanchard, Sheldon Bowles and Harvey Mackay

6. *Zap the Gaps*, by Kenneth H. Blanchard, Dana Gaines Robinson and James C. Robinson

7. *Execution*, by Larry Bossidy, Ram Charan and Charles Burck

8. *The New Leader's 100-Day Action Plan*, by George B. Bradt, Jayme A. Check and Jorge E. Pedraza

9. *Go Put Your Strengths to Work*, by Marcus Buckingham

10. *First, Break all the Rules*, by Marcus Buckingham and Curt Coffman

11. *Now, Discover Your Strengths*, by Marcus Buckingham and Donald O. Clifton

12. *StandOut*, by Marcus Buckingham.

13. *The Charge: Activating the 10 Human Drives That Make You Feel Alive*, by Brendon Burchard

14. *How to Stop Worrying and Start Living*,
    by Dale Carnegie

15. *The Ultimate Sales Machine*, by Chet Holmes,
    Jay Conrad Levinson and Michael Gerber

16. *The Leader's Digest*, by Jim Clemmer

17. *How the Mighty Fall*, by Jim Collins

18. *Good to Great*, by Jim Collins

19. *Built to Last*, Jim Collins and Jerry I. Porras

20. *Great by Choice*, by Jim Collins and Morten T. Hansen

21. *Rules for Renegades*, by Christine Comaford-Lynch

22. *The Oz Principle*, by Craig Hickman, Tom Smith
    and Roger Connors

23. *The 7 Habits of Highly Effective People*,
    by Stephen R. Covey

24. *The 8th Habit*, by Stephen R. Covey

25. *Strategic Speed*, by Jocelyn Davis, Henry M. Frechette
    and Edwin H. Boswell

26. *Six Thinking Hats*, by Edward de Bono

27. *Six Action Shoes*, by Edward de Bono

28. *Value-Creating Growth*, by Thomas L. Doorley III
    and John M. Donovan

29. *Serial Innovators: Firms That Change the World*,
    by Claudio Feser and Daniel Vasella

30. *Getting to Yes*, by Roger Fisher, William L. Ury
    and Bruce Patton

31. *The World is Flat*, by Thomas L. Friedman

32. *Execute... Or Be Executed*, by Sam Geist

33. *Blink*, by Malcolm Gladwell

34. *Soup: A Recipe to Nourish Your Team and Culture*, by Jon Gordon

35. *The Energy Bus*, by Jon Gordon and Ken Blanchard

36. *The No Complaining Rule*, by Jon Gordon

37. *The Shark and The Goldfish*, by Jon Gordon

38. *Training Camp*, by Jon Gordon

39. *The Seed: Finding Purpose and Happiness in Life and Work*, by Jon Gordon

40. *Reengineering the Corporation: A Manifesto for Business Revolution*, by Michael Hammer and James Champy

41. *Faster Cheaper Better: The 9 Levers for Transforming How Work Gets Done*, by Michael Hammer and Lisa Hershman

42. *Think and Grow Rich*, by Napoleon Hill

43. *POP!: Stand Out in Any Crowd*, by Sam Horn

44. *Steve Jobs: The Exclusive Biography*, by Walter Isaacson

45. *Iacocca: An Autobiography*, by Lee Iacocca with William Novak

46. *How Companies Win*, by Rick Kash and David Calhoun

47. *Blue Ocean Strategy*, by W. Chan Kim and Renee Mauborgne

48. *Leading Change*, by John P. Kotter

49. *What the Best CEOs Know*, by Jeffrey A. Krames

50. *The Power to Soar Higher*, by Peter Legge

51. *The Five Temptations of a CEO*, by Patrick Lencioni

52. *Silos, Politics, and Turf Wars*, by Patrick Lencioni

53. *The Five Dysfunctions of a Team*, by Patrick Lencioni

72. *Strengths Based Leadership*,
    by Tom Rath and Barry Conchie

73. *War in the Boardroom*, by Al Ries and Laura Ries

74. *The 22 Immutable Laws of Marketing*,
    by Al Ries and Jack Trout

75. *Leadership: A Treasury of Great Quotations
    for Those Who Aspire to Lead*,
    by William Safire and Leonard Safir

76. *You Don't Need a Title to Be a Leader*,
    by Mark Sanborn

77. *Your Management Sucks*, by Mark Stevens

78. *Power Retail: Winning Strategies from Chapters
    and Other Leading Retailers in Canada*,
    by Lawrence N. Stevenson, Joseph C. Shlesinger
    and Michael R. Pearce

79. *Leadership Above the Line*, by Sarah Sumner

80. *Now... Build A Great Business*, by Brian Tracy,
    Mark Thompson, and Frances Hesselbein

81. *Crunch Point*, by Brian Tracy

82. *Eat That Frog*, by Brian Tracy

83. *Focal Point*, by Brian Tracy

84. *Full Engagement*, by Brian Tracy

85. *Goals*, by Brian Tracy

86. *How The Best Leaders Lead*, by Brian Tracy

87. *The Art of Closing the Sale*, by Brian Tracy

88. *Turbo Coach*, by Brian Tracy and Campbell Fraser

89. *Trump: The Art of the Deal*, by Donald J. Trump
    and Tony Schwartz

90. *Off Balance on Purpose*, by Dan Thurmon

Aug. 25, 2013

# TOLEDO FREE ★ PRESS

**Opinion**

## A busy calendar, Autumn walking
Tom Pounds on upcoming philanthropy events and Michael S. Miller on a walking program at Metroparks.
**page 3**

## TedxToledo and cautionary words
Will Lucas on the 'ultimate brain spa' and Dr. Brian Hoeflinger on the cost of teenage drinking and driving.
**pages 4-5**

**Religion**

## 'A God thing'
CedarCreek Church fights human trafficking.
**page 10**

**Star**

## Downtown Jazz
Delfeayo Marsalis brings New Orleans to Grand Plaza Hotel.
**page 19**

Art Van Furniture

Business Link

# ART VAN '3.0'

CEO KIM YOST and ART VAN shake up local retail furniture market with innovative flagship store in Toledo. By Bailey G. Dick, **page 8**

213

NATIONAL HOME FURNISHINGS INDUSTRY
Anti-Defamation League
*'Protecting Our Future'*

July 11, 2013

Mr. Kim Yost
Chief Executive Officer
Art Van Furniture
6500 14 Mile Road
Warren, MI 48092

Dear Kim:

We were delighted to present you with the American Heritage Award at the 2013 National Home Furnishings Dinner. It is an honor to add a distinguished industry leader like you to our 'Family of Honorees'. Without a doubt, the evening was an outstanding success!

ADL is called upon daily to confront the dangerous enemies of freedom and justice. We must continually confront and challenge hateful speech and behavior. As this nation's premier civil rights/human relations agency fighting all forms of prejudice and bigotry, ADL's work to safeguard the democratic values we all hold dear is more important than ever.

Your support and participation is of immense value as you partner with us to spread awareness about ADL's work to a larger audience, while leading the way to our financial goal.

Thank you once again for supporting our efforts, we look forward to your participation in 2014!

Best regards,

*Neil*

Neil Goldberg
Raymour & Flanigan

*Joe*

Joe Laneve
Bloomingdales

Industry Co-Chairs

NG/JL:atb

605 Third Avenue · New York, NY 10158-3560
(212) 885-7885 / (212) 599-6988  bkatznelson@adl.org

# — Appendix C —

# PHOTO ALBUM

219

221